SURBITON MEMOR

& More tales of old Tolworth and Berrylands

*S*ince the Remembered series of books covering Tolworth, Hook, Chessington and Long Ditton were published, along with Surbiton Bombed, the author of these titles has acquired a wealth of new tales from the past provided by readers who want to share their memories and nostalgic pictures with others. Each week, the postman has arrived with mail from not just all over Britain but from around the world. The scores of envelopes and packages have contained a treasure trove of remarkable recollections, faded photos and stories of schooldays in Surbiton, trams in Tolworth, and life down on the farm in Long Ditton. Now, through the pages of this book, these tales of a bygone era can be shared by other readers and a new generation of young people keen to find out more about the area where they now live and how it has changed so much.

Eric Stickley, Tom the horse and Tiny the dog in Victoria Road, Surbiton, on a hot day in 1950.

Town trio in the 1950s

DURING the early 1950s, a familiar sight in Surbiton town centre was that of a trio — Tiny the dog, Tom the horse, and 20-year-old Eric Stickley. Eric worked for his family who ran a contracting business at Hook Road and carried out much work for Surbiton Borough Council.

Tom pulled the cart, which was never known to leave without Tiny, a mongrel found in Hook Road during the Second World War.

In spite of the jolting he received, Tiny stayed at the front of the cart with his forefeet resting on the headboard. In 1950, Eric told the Surrey Comet: "There is such a bond between the two animals that I doubt if one would leave for work without the other."

Besides being company for the horse, Tiny had another job — he guarded the cart and its contents when Eric was away. And he apparently carried out this responsible task most effectively.

Famous nature writer

Richard Jefferies and Woodside 60 years after he left.

A YOUNG nature writer whose wonderful essays were published in a series of books, spent five years living with his family in Tolworth. Richard Jefferies' home was at No 2 Woodside, (later better known as No 296 Ewell Road) where he resided with his wife, Jessie, son Richard, and daughter, also Jessie.

Jefferies, a journalist born in Wiltshire in 1849, lived at the villa close to today's Douglas Road, from 1877-1882. He died in 1887 aged 38. The author loved the open countryside around Hook, Tolworth and Claygate, where he spent many hours observing wildlife. He wrote that the first spring he lived in Surrey, he was "astonished and delighted" by the variety of birdlife, which included large numbers of nightingales and "bevies of chiff-chaffs and willow wrens." His favourite spot was the bridge which carried Kingston Road over the river near Tolworth Court Farm.

One of his essays talks about the trout in the river at Tolworth.

Special thanks

Alan Davis   Doreen Conroy   Paul Adams   Winnie Randall   Martin Summers

Front cover pictures: Victoria Road, Surbiton, in the early 1960s (left); St Mark's Hill, Surbiton and the 281 Routemaster bus in the 1970s (right); and Tolworth Broadway in about 1959 (below).

Acknowledgments

Paul Adams, Pat Grinter, Steve Fay, Dennis Stickley, Gay Taylor, Lorna Thompson, Reg Driver, 'Digger' Arculus, Tony Cornell, Doreen Conroy (née Wells), George Benham and family; Joe Buckingham, Joyce and Eddie Gardner, Marion Knocks, Jill Lamb, Emma and staff at Local History Room, North Kingston Centre, Royal Borough of Kingston; Lady D. Stack and family; Winnie Randall, Eileen Stone, Barbara Owen, public relations office at Stoke Park, Caroline Bott, M. Deadman, J. Atkins, B and N Horrocks, Janet Ellingworth, Rod Jones, Beryl Havers, Joan Hynes, Christine Wright, Kate Poole, Peggy Schutters, T Boyd, Maura Collard, Ingrid and Garth Holford, Jim Ingram, Alan Davis, John Rook, John Oborn, Paul Muggleton, Martin Summers, Pat Harman, Maureen Weedon, Wendy Buller, Mr and Mrs R. Glass, Patricia Bamber, Dr J. Longhurst, Frank Trigg, Ron Ingram, Mr S. Chamberlain and staff of The Hollyfield School, Nigel Davison, Susan Vaughan, M and N Davison, Marion Bone, P.F. Butler, Colin Prendergast, David Tippett Wilson, P. Clarke, Christine Malthouse, Alfred D'Araujo, Martin R Draper (great-grandson of William David Hughes) who sadly passed away on 23rd August 2004, Ray Lloyd for unceasing encouragement and Doreen Huggett for the unexpected cream tea during research work.

Photograph credits

Mark Davison collection, Dennis Stickley, Reg Driver collection, Gay Taylor's Broom family collection; Zerstorer Gruppe book (German airmen casualties); Doreen Conroy (née Wells); Digger Arculus collection, Leslie Sandler, Farewell To London's Trolleybuses; Lady D. Stack's personal collection; Eileen Stone, Express Newspapers, Caroline Bott collection, Kingston Local History Studies, Janet Ellingworth, Beryl Horrocks, Rod Jones collection, Beryl Havers, Jim Ingram, Alan Davis collection, Martin Summers, Kingston Local History Room, Music Week, Stuart Andrews and Wendy Buller.

Bibliography

Surbiton Borough guides (various); estate agents' brochures; After the Battle magazine; Surrey Comet; Kingston Borough News; The Life and Works of Alfred Bestall by Caroline G Bott; Daily Express; Nature Near London; A Worthing Cavalcade; The Story of Kingston by June Sampson. Surbiton Past by Richard Statham; Kingston Then and Now by Margaret Bellars; All Change, by June Sampson; Tolworth Remembered by Mark Davison and Paul Adams; Hook Remembered Again by Mark Davison; Kelly's directories, various years; Zerstorer Gruppe book; Farewell To London's Trolleybuses; Surbiton – Thirty-Two Years Of Self-Government by Rowley Richardson.

**Published by Mark Davison
North Bank, Smoke Lane, Reigate,
Surrey RH2 7HJ.
Tel: 01737 221215
e-mail: mark.davison1@virgin.net**

Copyright 2004   ISBN 0-9543759-1-2

First edition October 2004

**Printed by Litho Techniques (Kenley),
Godstone Road, Whyteleafe, Surrey.**

Trolley bus wires criss-cross Claremont Road, Surbiton, in the 1950s. This bustling street opposite Surbiton Station is one of the town's busiest roads. The old Odeon, not visible in the picture, was on the left, set back. It closed for good on 8th February 1975 and in modern times has been redeveloped as a Waitrose supermarket. The clocktower, designed to commemorate the coronation of Edward VII in August 1902, was erected in 1908, just two years before the king died. It had taken six years to raise the money.

THE BROADWAY, TOLWORTH.   TL 51

Tolworth Roundabout in the 1950s. Some elderly people recall a pond at this location before the roundabout was constructed. The Kingston bypass was built in the late 1920s and was one of the first in Britain. It stretched from Kingston Vale to Hinchley Wood. By the late 1950s the amount of traffic had increased dramatically. Gone were the days children would sit at the corner on Sunday afternoons watching the occasional motor car pass by. The A3 Tolworth underpass was built in 1967. The Odeon was pulled down in February 1961 and the 22-storey Tolworth Tower was built in its place. Among the many wireless masts now on the Tower's roof are those used by Radio Jackie, whose studios in the old main Post Office building in The Broadway opened in October 2003.

Most of the grand villas along the Portsmouth Road by Queen's Promenade have not survived to the modern day, although one or two remained into the new century. Dr Thomas Barnardo, the philanthropic founder of the children's homes, lived in retirement at St Leonard's Lodge, No 51 Portsmouth Road, at the corner of St Leonard's Road. He died at the house in 1905. Later, a Barnardo's home for boys was opened in what is the Blenheim Gardens area of Kingston Hill, near Kingston Hospital.

Charles Lowe & Co.,
Dispensing Chemists.

Opposite the Station, SURBITON.

ESTABLISHED 1848.

Best Quality only. Lowest Prices.

An advert for Lowe's, No 1 Claremont Road, Surbiton, in about 1902.

Chemist Charles Lowe's house, Devon Villa, No 15 Hook Road, pictured in the year 2002. He lived there in the late 1870s and 1880s until his death.

Chemist's cure for sore throats

Famous lozenges

CHARLES Lowe, born in Hackney, London, in 1831, kept this chemist's at No 1 Claremont Road, Surbiton, during the 1870s, but after his retirement while still in his fifties, it continued to keep the family name well into the 20th century.

Mr Lowe lived at Devon Villa, (now No 15) Hook Road, from 1877 until his death in the 1880s.

He had taken over the villa from Frederick Thuell, a well-respected man from Exeter who was a prominent member of St Paul's Church, Hook.

After his death, Mr Lowe's widow, Susannah, who was brought up in Scotland, continued to live for many years at Devon Villa.

Three years before they arrived in Hook Road, the Lowes' next door neighbours at St David's, 13 Hook Road, were the famous author Thomas Hardy and his wife, Emma, who were in residence from October 1874 to March 1875.

Their old home, renamed Holmbury Cottage in 1876, was pulled down in 1960 and Midhurst Court flats was built on the site.

In his promotional material for the chemist's, Mr Lowe wrote of his own brand Lowe's Celebrated Lozenges:

"Upwards of 30 years' experience with the testimony of many of the most eminent of the medical profession has fully confirmed the reputation of these lozenges."

In the year 2004, Winnie Randall recalled being taken by her mother as a young girl to Lowe's in about 1920 from the family home in Cleaveland Road.

"We went in there to get cough mixture and Mum would also buy Pompeian cream – a face powder. She used to have a beautiful face. Sometimes she bought Indian scent."

Charles Lowe had this chemist's at No 1 Claremont Road, Surbiton. It offered curious cures.

CLAREMONT RD SURBITON

2488

Charles Lowe's chemist's at No 1 Claremont Road, Surbiton, shortly before the 1914-18 war. A flat-capped "sandwich board man" is pacing up and down the entrance to Surbiton Station advertising films showing at the Coronation Hall. On this particular day, A Woman's Crime was being screened. On the left of the picture, Nightingale Phillips and Page, auctioneers is heavily advertised. Above the chemist's shop is a sign saying that there is a public telephone on the premises. In the window are signs advertising lemonade and ginger ale available to thirsty customers "in syphons". Tram wires began to criss-cross the skyline here in 1906.

Picturesque in the golden September sun

Happy days on the farm at Ditton Hill

TAKE a walk down leafy Love Lane at the top of Herne Road, and after a few hundred yards you will come across a Victorian farmhouse still surrounded by fields alongside the Kingston bypass. Today it is no longer a farm but is still a residence. Originally this was Hill Farm, later known as Ditton Hill Farm. Some may remember it was also called Broom Farm, after the family name of the farmers. It boasted a herd of 60 cows.

Originally from Culmstock, Devon, the Brooms came to Surrey in about 1900, taking over not just Hill Farm, Ditton Hill, but also Sondes Place Farm, Dorking.

Harry Richard Broom, who ran Ditton Hill Farm, was one of seven children of John and Louisa Broom. His grand-daughter, Gay, born in 1932, remembers many happy times spent on the farm.

From her home in retirement at Chandlers Ford, Hampshire, she recalled that the farm was "elegant in its grey stature and picturesque in the golden September sun." The brightly-coloured leaves of the Virginia creeper would look resplendent on the old brick, she said.

Originally, the farmhouse had tall and elaborately-fashioned chimneys but Gay's grandparents had them removed after severe gales in about 1914 and shorter chimneys replaced them. The roof was high with grey slate.

The winding path to the farmhouse was lined by lilac rhododendron bushes and near the drawing room windows was a large circular holly. By the door was a brass foot scraper and a brass door knocker and letter box. A sweeping lawn surrounded by large laurels spread down to the meadows and a blue wooden summer-house with a thatched roof stood in the grounds. In the spring the flower beds were a mass of daffodils and in late summer buckets of plums and apples were put out for sale.

Just after the First World War, the farm's cowman was Fred Driver, who lived in Haycroft Road.

Harry Broom and his wife, Kate, moved out of the farm in 1953 marking the end of an era.

Lorna Broom, one of the five children of Harry and Kate Broom, was born at Ditton Hill Farm in 1914 and at the age of 90 was living just a few miles away in Molesey.

Lorna Broom attending to the horses.

Horses plough the fields at Ditton Hill.

Fred Driver with one of Harry Broom's shire horses.

Puzzle over dead in Messerschmitt crash

MORE than 60 years after a two-seater Messerschmitt ME110 was shot down in flames by fighters near Tolworth Court Farm, the mystery of the number of German casualties remains.

Surbiton Mortuary recorded that three died, one being D.R.K. Gelferin, aged 23, of No 30 Wielandstrasse, Frankfurt. The other two were aged 19 and 20.

The book, The Battle of Britain Then and Now, states that only Uffz. Pfafflhuber and gunner Uffz. Kramp, a radio operator, perished. They served with the German regiment 15 Staffel.

Military historians have carried out much research over the years to determine the true story of the fate of the Messerschmitt which fell out of the sky and buried itself in the Maori sports ground cricket field, behind Kingston Road, on 9th September 1940.

The badly burnt and mutilated body parts presented crash investigators and undertakers with a difficult task.

Latest research suggests that there were only two victims after all. It is felt that a letter possibly found among the possessions of one of the victims gave his girlfriend's address in Germany and that she may have been the equivalent of a Red Cross worker (Deutches Rotes Kreux or D.R.K.). In the confusion after the crash, her details were wrongly thought to be that of a third young German airman.

Even more odd is that some historians claim that D.R.K

German airman Uffz Alois Pfafflhuber.

Gelferin was, in fact, the name of a German airman in another Messerschmitt ME110 which came down at Woodcote Park, near Epsom. He suggests that because the Maori ground has a Worcester Park address, the bodies may have gone firstly to Epsom, hence the understandable confusion that arose.

Researchers have been to Frankfurt in a bid to ascertain the truth and a letter was published in a German newspaper to no avail.

The Woodcote Park crash victim, it transpired, was named Ostermunchner and all three men are buried in adjacent graves at the German war cemetery at Cannock Chase, Staffordshire.

Anthony Cornell was one of those keen to learn the truth. He said it could not be ruled out that since the "Gelferin" body was not registered at Surbiton Mortuary until September 15, it may be that a body part had been found in nearby trees some days after the crash together with fragments of the letter from his girlfriend.

"My guess is that the body part was from Kramp, as Pfaffelhuber was known for being very attached to a girl in his home town in Austria. Kramp had amused his fellow airmen by playing tunes on a violin next to her photo."

Killed: Uffz. Otto Kramp.

A year after the crash, a German Luftwaffe forage cap was found in a tree by Maori gardener, Mr Dare.

The three Allied airmen who brought down the Germans were private officer Norman Tamblyn, a Canadian of 242 Squadron (shot down and killed in 1941 two days after receiving the Distinguished Flying Cross from the King); flying officer Stanoslav Pejfar, a Czech of 310 Squadron (later shot down and killed in a close-escort operation in Boulogne in 1942); and private officer Vaclav Bergman, also a Czech of 310 Squadron. He survived the war and was also awarded the Distinguished Flying Cross.

Peggy Brown's cake shop

PEGGY Brown's cake shop at Claremont Road is remembered affectionately by many Surbiton people. It was run by an Australian lady and sold delicious home-made cakes. There were wonderful window displays. Inside, dolls, toys and various characters were perched among the madeleines, scones and Victoria sponges.

It was a mouth-watering treat for visitors to stand and enjoy the lavish presentation and try to choose a confection. The premises were at 12-16 Claremont Road.

Grotesque figure mystery

The frightening statue as recalled by Doreen Conroy.

A MYSTERIOUS grotesque figure mounted on a plinth scared many a schoolchild in the 1930s and 1940s outside Evans, the chemist, No 3 Hook Road, opposite the Maypole public house. The black-coloured statue had huge feet and its face was severe. Some mischievous youngsters used to place a cigarette in its mouth or cover the private parts with a leaf. The purpose of the display is a puzzle. The old-fashioned chemist appears to have been opened in 1927 by Evans Stafford Ltd, drug stores and run by Richard Evans who also had a branch at No 29 Surbiton Road, Kingston.

Serving Sir Rowland at Wentworth, Ditton Hill

George Benham at Wentworth, Ditton Hill. He was the chauffeur for Sir Rowland Hodge.

On Ditton Hill, close to the junction with Herne Road, stood a grand old house called Wentworth. It was pulled down in the 1930s and the name is recalled in the development which was built on the site — Wentworth Close. Before its demise, Wentworth was the home in the 1920s of Sir Rowland Hodge (born 1859) a prominent shipbuilder on Tyneside and managing director for 20 years of the Northumberland Shipbuilding Company. He had moved to Long Ditton from Chipstead Place, near Sevenoaks, Kent and brought some of his staff with him. They included head chauffeur, Mr Wicks and another driver, George Benham. The shipping magnate sold Wentworth to developers and moved to Churt, near Farnham, where he renamed his new house Chipstead.

Mr Benham stayed in the area and at 90 was living in Fircroft Road, Hook. His brother-in-law, Les Green, ran the White Hart, Hook, in the 1970s.

Chauffeur Wicks with Sir Rowland's young sons.

Chauffeur George with Sir Rowland's Rolls.

Work begins on constructing Tolworth Tower in 1961. The Toby Jug is in the background.

Building work starts on a subway crossing in Tolworth Broadway.

My Tolworth memories

Childhood days in Tolworth in the 1930s will never be forgotten by Arthur 'Digger' Arculus, even though for much of his adult life he has resided in New Zealand. In retirement 12,000 miles away from 'home', he has looked back fondly on his Surbiton days as an adventurous schoolboy.

Digger's father, also called Arthur, was born in 1902 and died in 1998 and his mother, May (née Hunt) was born in 1901, the year that Queen Victoria died. She passed away in 1978. At the age of three, in 1929, Digger and his parents moved to Tolworth from Fulham in London just after his father commenced work at Hawker Aircraft Company at Canbury Park Road, Kingston, in December that year as a fitter.

Digger wrote: "No. 45 Ravenswood Avenue was purchased for £525 and the deposit needed was £50. Dad had a hard job to find this deposit but made it up with £25 borrowed and the rest was very hard earned doing other jobs in the evenings. Repayment for the mortgage was £4 6s 0d a month at six per cent for 20 years."

Digger's uncle, Harry Hunt, born in 1903, who worked at Vickers Armstrongs at Weybridge as the toolroom foreman and his Aunt Winn moved into 33 Ravenswood Avenue at about the same time.

"Having moved into the house after trials and tribulations getting some jobs put right, we then had a problem of a very big tree trunk in our front garden just where the front wall would go against a pavement. The builders who should have put a wall up went bust and Dad had to get the tree trunk out before a wall could be built by himself.

"Incidentally, Ravenswood Avenue had not been built at this time, and my father once wrote in a diary he kept: 'Truly rural, in fact, I remember we could walk across fields to Epsom and Chessington.'

Arthur senior also wrote that children counted the rings on the offending tree trunk and found it could have been 250 years old.

Digger junior continues the story: "Having commenced digging, my father looked up and saw nine other blokes had arrived with various tools and wedges, cross-cut saws and the like, offering to assist. My mother opened the windows and

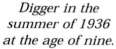

Digger in the summer of 1936 at the age of nine.

Digger and wife Barbara in 1950. They were married at St Matthew's Church in July 1949.

got the gramophone going — a forerunner of music while you work? Big hunks of wood were taken away for winter burning.

"Dad wrote that it was a happy community and night after night always saw several chaps reducing the tree stump until we finally got it out and hauled it into the middle of the unmade road, where it was used by many a courting couple.

"My father wrote that when the building firm, Fearnlea Building Co, had the receivers in, my uncle Harry, Mr Pat Carter of 49 Ravenswood Avenue, Mr Harry Lamb at No. 47 and my father got together and formed the Ravenswood Avenue Association and decided for all of us to put half a crown (2s 6d) in the kitty and get Harry Hunt's friend, a solicitor, to look after our interests, otherwise we could see the added expense of having to pay road and paving charges which of course we had thought was already taken care of.

"This was about the time I almost drowned in The Bluey which was a water-filled quarry of the local brick building firm, near Fullers Way. How it got this name I do not know. I remember it was Good Friday and I had gone with some other

boys across to The Bluey and I told my parents that 'I just stepped on a log and it went down'.

"The boy who saved me was one of the 'Pompy' boys. I wish to this day that I could remember his real name."

"The Bluey was very deep indeed and sadly there had been one or two drownings there, plus a mention of a steamroller having gone down at some time or other.

"A gentleman with the name of Piggett, I believe, used to keep an eye on children and was employed as a caretaker by the brickfield company. He would chase any of us he saw getting close to the place. Needless to say his nickname was Piggy.

"We used to have a lot of fun around that place, but it didn't pay to be caught by Piggy, believe me.

"Back to 45 Ravenswood and my father had now to build a front wall. He told me he had permission (I hope) to take some of the bricks at the end of the road, so off we went with the wheelbarrow and picked up some bricks, then someone taught him how to lay them correctly and in the end we had a very nice wall with three piercaps which dad made up a mould for. The wall lasted many years with only a slight sinking in the centre due to the settlement over the years from the hole of the tree trunk. I remember the wall standing well up to 1979 and later on I received a photo of the front of the house, now modernised and the new wall of the same design with piercaps as well. I was pleased about that.

"In about 1931 when I was five, I commenced school at the Red Lion/Douglas Road School. My education was somewhat curtailed due to bronchitis as whenever the winter came along I suffered from this complaint and it took its toll over the years until I served in the Middle East when the sun and climate cured my chest for ever.

Arthur senior and May Arculus on holiday at Box Hill during the Second World War.

Teachers there were always helpful but unfortunately I was never academically minded, even at that early age and preferred the outdoor life to study. Mrs Rootes was one lady I remember well. Another, whose name I cannot remember, married a teacher, Mr Moody, from the Tolworth Central School, who later became headmaster at the Red Lion Road school when I met him in the mid 1950s.

"During my time at this school I had some trouble with a front tooth that grew inwards and had to attend Great Ormond Street Hospital in London. The result of this was that for a time I had to wear a form of plate with an elastic band hooked across it. If that elastic band came adrift I had to go home and my mother had a special hook to get it back in place.

"One thing that made the elastic band come off was to eat bonbons. This antic was a marvellous way to be excused lessons and be able to go home. This was until my mother, always wise to my tricks, showed the teacher, Mrs Rootes, how to put the elastic band back in place. Oh well, you can't win them all.

"Red Lion Road was quite a busy road in its own way during those years, with horses and carts travelling from the brick fields, I believe, to dump their waste somewhere. We children used to try and cadge a ride by hanging on to the back without the driver knowing.

"Then there was the first drain suction vehicle, very similar to those used in present times. We children used to follow these around from drain to drain, fascinated with its operation.

"Another rather dangerous occupation was when the Sunlight laundry van came down the road and some children used to run in front of it to make the driver sound his musical horn. It is a wonder that none of us were killed, either by the van or by a parent who saw it happen.

"I still have an octagonal medal struck for the occasion of the Borough of Surbiton Charter Day in 1936. It is of a dark chocolate colour with a royal blue coloured ribbon. One side of the medal is inscribed 'Borough of Surbiton Charter Day 16 September 1936 — 1855-1936'.

"The other side has the crest of the borough. I was just under 11 at the time and us schoolchildren paraded up at Hollyfield Road, by the Fishponds at the bottom of the hill in Ewell Road, and marched up to the council offices."

Digger said various people and places around Surbiton often sprang to mind when he started reminiscing.

Laurie Tilbury, of the Tilbury cake shop on the corner of Princes Road and Ewell Road on the Broadway, was one such person. When Digger returned to England for a visit in 1998,

Princes Avenue, Tolworth in about 1930.

he was greatly saddened to see the premises in a state of disrepair.

Digger remembers Alan Aird being bombed out of his home in Oakley Avenue. He married a girl called Doreen and is believed to have moved away later to Norfolk.

Others were vividly recalled, too. Eddy Cranford lived at No 44 Ravenswood Avenue and, had a sister Elsie. Eddy married and moved to Kitchener, Ontario, Canada. He and his wife Joan, were still living in Kitchener in 2003.

Derek Painter lived at 95 Princes Avenue. Digger met him at a camp in the Troodos Mountains, Cyprus, when on leave from Palestine in 1946, and then again back in Tolworth after the war, in 1948.

John Halfhead lived in Princes Avenue, near the Broadway end of the road. His parents had a lot to do with the 2nd Tolworth Scouts.

Derek Fraser's home was in Ravenswood Avenue near the Cranborne Avenue end. He trained to be a navigator in the RAF in Rhodesia.

Brian Ansell was the son of the owner of the Ansell piano shop on the Broadway. Digger said he believed it was he who purchased No 44 Ravenswood Avenue, Eddy Cranford's former

house, when he married.

Mr Kerslake was another teacher at Tolworth Central School. Digger met him again during the war after leaving school when Mr Kerslake taught maths at 1345 ATC Squadron at its Beverley Road school headquarters in New Malden.

"He helped me a lot with my maths before my Air Crew Selection Board at Cardington in March 1944.

"His words on meeting me again at ATC were: 'Ah, young Arculus, we meet again, I have no stick this time!' We became quite good pals thereafter."

Another teacher from the Red Lion School Digger recalls was Mrs Rootes, a "nice person".

Maureen Lock lived at the Royston Court flats along the Kingston bypass. Then, her family moved into a house at the top of Tolworth Rise, damaged by a bomb on 9th September 1940.

"I believe the family was related to the Locks Antique shop people in Ripley village."

Digger was also friends with the two daughters of the manager of Mac Fisheries in the Broadway, as well as the daughter of the owner of Frank's, the ladies' hat shop also in the Broadway near the Red Lion public house.

More schoolboy memories of Tolworth

Close to the Council Offices at the top of Ewell Road was the school clinic, dentist's and the like. "The clinic has very poignant memories for me after one of my schoolboy exploits," writes Digger Arculus, who lived in Ravenswood Avenue, Tolworth.

"Our mothers had a lot to contend with when we were younger, didn't they? Such as mine when I came home after playing in a field where there was an old rusty wrecked lorry. We were having a stone fight and I jumped through the door of this lorry and tore my left leg at the hip. It wouldn't stop bleeding and when I was taken to the doctor he poured from one of those large iodine bottles to stop the bleeding.

The outcome was that I got iodine poisoning which turned into impetigo and I had sores all over my knees and chin.

At the hospital there was even talk of having the leg off. Mum wouldn't have that so she took me to the school clinic up near the Surbiton Library and they had a look at it and said they may be able to do something. Within a week things were coming right at last. We were a trial weren't we?

I and many others owe a lot to that clinic but I can well remember screaming children heading for the dentist's there.

An event that took place before the war in a field on the Esher side of the Ace of Spades roundabout at Hook was the annual Alan Cobham's air displays. These always pulled in the crowds.

One day I and many others went down to have a look. This turned into a very sad day.

In those days the parachutist would be towed from the wing of an aeroplane after he had pulled at his ripcord. But on this occasion, the parachute failed to deploy.

Being a typical lad I went rushing around to the field in which the parachutist had come down, and someone sensibly stopped us at the gate.

I remember the parachutist was carried through that gate, and I understand that he died some days later. It must have been about 1938 or possibly 1939. Believe me it has remained in my memory for all these years.

Derby Day caused great traffic jams at the Tolworth roundabout by Fox and Nicholls, the Toby Jug, the Odeon and Garlicks sweet shop after the races. One of

Ewell Road, Tolworth behind what is now The Broadway, in the 1930s.

the things I took part in, very much against my mother's wishes, was to stand beside the roundabout with other children and call out: 'Throw out your mouldy coppers!' Believe me we made quite a bit doing that and immediately, as the money burnt a hole in our pockets, rushed over to Garlicks to purchase some sweets. I got into trouble for taking part in this, but I did take mum a bar of chocolate as a peace offering.

While on the subject of shops, there was Linegars the sweet shop in Red Lion Road where I used to belong to the Firework Club. A halfpenny here and a penny there slowly made up a princely sum for firework night.

Next door to Linegars was the fish shop run by a family called Shill. It was I believe a large family and one of the older sons ran a dance band. Unfortunately he started to go blind and a large article was written in the Surrey Comet about him. Wonderful fish and chips were sold there.

Then came the war years. I think it was very early on, possibly 1939 when riding in a tram from Surbiton, on top, in the front seat of course, when reaching Hollyfield Road (The Fishponds) on the way down the hill I spotted my first barrage balloon. This was from the RAF Hook Barrage Balloon Training Centre. It was from there that they

used to bring a barrage balloon on a truck to the fields across the Kingston bypass for positioning training.

Later on I was over the fields with some other lads when one of these training operations was taking place. They would have the balloon at a very low height from the truck and then slowly drive from one field to another.

One rather windy day during one of these trips a gust of wind skewed the balloon into one of the trees as it was being towed through a gateway from one field to another. It hit the tree and tore open and deflated, whereupon a million, well quite a few, children descended on the ripped balloon and gathered bits of the fabric.

I got a piece that was large enough to cover Dad's motorcycle combination that was parked at the side of the house.

I am afraid I still feel remorse for the poor Flight Sergeant who must have taken just the piece of string that tethered the balloon back to the Hook base. He must have been put on a charge, poor fellow. He didn't stand an earthly with all those children about.

I spoke of the trams that were on the run at Tolworth. I would like to deviate a little and mention that my Grandfather Arculus was one of the first six tram drivers in London and I still have his bone whistle that he used later as a regulator. He was made a regulator after having been pulled up twice for speeding! I still have my first ration book made out to the general store of Chesters just into Thornhill Road from Red Lion Road. Nellie Chester, a kindly soul, used to run this shop while her brother Lionel had the off licence next to it.

I often laughed as Nellie would offer something different to what you wanted if she hadn't got the item you asked for. To the request 'A pot of paste please' she would reply 'Sorry, we haven't any pots of paste, but I do have some baking powder'. Other than that it was such a well-run shop.

We were off school for a very long time as the shelters had not been built by the time the war commenced. This was wonderful for us children playing down by the Hogsmill, shooting the rapids on rafts and the like. The main result of this was the loss of schooling. After some of the shelters were built, one side for boys and the other for girls, someone hit a cricket ball and it hit the overhang of the top of the surface shelter. This overhang was about three inches thick and the ball chipped quite a large piece out of it, much to the delight of the children. An omen, perhaps.

While on the subject of these shelters, which ran down the centre of the playing field, one of the days during the Battle of Britain we had to spend from very early afternoon until something like 6.30pm as the all-clear hadn't sounded. Mothers brought down packets of biscuits and other foodstuff for us. Eventually we were allowed to run home and also allowed to climb over the fence beside the Kingston bypass as it was the shortest way home.

On Friday 18 October 1940 I was out in the playing field and a Spitfire (P3931) I later learned was piloted by private officer P.E.G.Carter, went on to crash at Kempton Park racecourse. Carter flew very low overhead and was wobbling very badly. I remember he was partially out of the cockpit at the time obviously looking for somewhere to crash-land, but there were too many people in the playing field. I cannot remember for certain if I had observed smoke from the aircraft but he flew on out of my sight and jumped out of the aircraft at 50ft without his parachute, and the aircraft crashed in Kempton Park racecourse. Sadly Carter was killed.

In all, his Polish squadron based at Northolt lost four pilots. The other three killed were private officers Wapniarek (P3872) and J.Borowski who crashed at high speed and burnt out on the racecourse near to Carter. A.Zukowski (V6571) crashed at Bluebell Hill. All for a possible loss of a Ju88 aircraft. Another sad memory of mine.

During the Battle of Britain those of us in our last year at school had the job of ringing a school bell when we heard the air-raid sirens. One would sit outside the school and listen for the northern command sirens then ring the bell if we heard them. The snag was that the Kingston bypass bordered the southern and northern commands, therefore it was not always easy to tell which sirens did sound. So there was a racket that sometimes went on. For a few farthings one would ring the bell and everyone would run to the shelters, but sometimes there was a deliberate false alarm to gain an extra farthing. This was soon found out and was stopped very abruptly after the cane had been administered. By the way, a farthing would get you a nice Trebor sweet. That was before sweets went on ration.

Talking of sweet rationing, that came in later. One could pur-

Ewell Road, Surbiton Hill, in the 1930s showing the Methodist Church, constructed in 1881-2. The church is built from red Leicester brick. It replaced an iron church put up in 1876 which sat 450 people. On the right, behind the garden trees is a sign advertising John Coleman's veterinary surgery. Inset: Digger at camp in 1938.

chase from a chemist shop a stick of Spanish liquorice without coupons. It acted like a very strong laxative. I for one found that you could pass it around the family and no one else would dream of touching it. As I enjoyed liquorice, and still do, except sweet things are now out of bounds unfortunately, this assisted me during the sweet rationing. Boy were they strong liquorice sticks."

Surbiton Urban District Council offices, Ewell Road, Surbiton Hill in 1936. A sign points to Surbiton Lagoon.

In the early 20th century, horse buses ran between Surbiton and Putney.

Trolleybuses first ran from Twickenham to Tolworth via Kingston and Surbiton in July 1931. Their last trip was on 8th May 1962.

The 602 trolleybus ferried passengers on a route between North Kingston and Winters Bridge, Long Ditton (pictured here).

Mountcoombe Hotel's heyday

Oakhill's villas

AMONG the grand old Victorian villas which stand proudly in Surbiton's leafy Oakhill area is The Sanctuary, formerly The Mountcoombe Hotel. Set in three acres of delightful grounds, which included a croquet lawn, tennis courts and sweeping gardens, the hotel provided rooms for visitors to the town from 1915 to the 1950s.

Mountcoombe stood on the south side of Oakhill Grove next to the junction with Oak Hill and in the late 1930s offered "the largest and best situated hotel in the district".

As well as "first-class catering" there were "bedrooms with hot and cold running water", according to an advertisement in 1938 (*right, below*).

The facilities included two tennis courts, billiards, bridge and dancing.

In the picture (*right*), deckchairs can be seen dotted around the garden on a summer's day and one of the lawns is equipped for games of croquet.

A new annexe offered "sunbathing roofs" and "rooms fitted with hot and cold water". Central heating had just been completed.

It would appear that the original Mountcoombe house was converted to a hotel during the First World War.

In the years leading up to its conversion it was the home of Jesse Ratcliffe.

Originally, the building was a mansion, Oak Hill Lodge, built in about 1880 for Arthur Bryant, from the renowned Bryant and May matches firm. Arthur's brother, Wilberforce Bryant, had another mansion, The

The Mountcoombe Hotel and its grounds. Note the croquet lawn and deckchairs.

Gables, built for him in South Bank, Surbiton, in the same period. The Gables later became Hillcroft College when the establishment relocated from Beckenham in 1926.

In 1912, neighbours of Mountcoombe on the south side of Oakhill Grove included A.H. Rand, in Oak Hill Cottage, and Gerald Wray in Adare. Another property, The Cottage, could be found before the junction with Walpole Road.

By 1916, the premises was being run by Mountcoombe Ltd and was advertised as a private hotel.

Neighbours at the time included Albert Hoare, who lived at a house called Ivanhoe.

By 1932, the hotel was owned by H. F. Reed who was still the proprietor during the Second World War. In 1940, immediate neighbours included Arthur Nugent at No 5 and Charles Edgar Shelley at No 3. A Mrs Tanner was living at No 1 just before the war.

By 1951, the old hotel had become the home of the National Young Life Campaign Training College of Evangelism.

The hotel is recalled in the name of Mountcombe Close — only one "o" — a smart estate of houses and flats constructed at the top of Upper Brighton Road, Surbiton, in the late 1960s.

For at least three decades, the old Mountcoombe hotel has been used as offices for about a dozen different businesses.

The building is now called The Sanctuary and in the year 2004, still stood gracefully atop Oakhill Grove. From its upper windows expansive views across the South East could be enjoyed.

Long since gone are its three acres of grounds. Short lawns and small copses are all that remain. The old gardens have been used since the Second World War for housing development but across the road the wooded bird sanctuary was preserved.

This wood was laid out by Surbiton's borough council at a cost of £2,500 in the early 1950s. On the upper slopes is the bird sanctuary, known as Jefferies' Wood, in memory of the Victorian naturalist and writer, Richards Jefferies, who lived at Woodside, Ewell Road, Tolworth — between the Douglas Road and the Worthington Road junctions. The wood was once part of the grounds of The Gables (Hillcroft College).

As a girl, Joyce Eggleton and her pals used to play in the wood, then private. One day, in the late 1920s, they were exploring the copse and light-heartedly rehearsing school plays.

An elderly man appeared and shouted out: 'What are you doing? You mustn't be here, you know'.

Joyce said the palings around the wood were broken and there was a gap through which they got inside the spinney. The man went on to tell them it belonged to a private house.

On another occasion Joyce and her friend had spotted a grave for a dead sparrow in the higher part of the wood.

In the first decade of the 21st century, some of the old villas in Oakhill were still standing. Their address was The Parade in mid-Victorian times.

No 1 (Elmside), a three-storey mansion with a basement, built next to Oakhill Path, was being used by Kingston NHS Primary Care Trust in 2004. Next door, No 2, was still called Inverbrae, and was smartly renovated and painted cream. Its gardens were lined with rhododendron bushes. Both Elmside and Inverbrae were names used for these houses in the 1880s, soon after they were built.

In the late 1880s, the Clowes family lived at Inverbrae and James Case at Elmside.

For some years around 1970, Elmside was used as the Surbiton Hospital nurses' home, while Inverbrae was the home, in that same period, of Norman Latchford, Alan Brown, Cyril Nightingale and Gilbert Price. In 1934, a flat in Inverbrae was the home of a retired churchman. The Reverend

The luxurious Oak Hill Lodge, which became Mountcoombe Hotel, Oak Hill Grove, in 1915.

William Thomas Martin studied for a theological degree at Durham and was ordained as a priest in 1889. He was curate of a church in Bexleyheath from 1888-1891, curate of Eccleshill, Yorkshire, 1891-1893 and in Yalding from 1894-1897. He then took positions in Rusthall, Kent, 1897-1899 and Goudhurst from 1900-1903 before becoming rector of Bicknor and Huckinge from 1904-1915.

Another cleric also lived in Oak Hill in the 1930s — the Reverend Wilson Griffiths Brougham Butlin MA.

Mr Butlin was ordained as a priest in 1885 and took up his first position as curate of Camden Church, Camberwell, in 1885. From 1890 to 1897 he was vicar of Donnington, after which until 1903, he held the post of rector of Wardleigh, Oakhampton, Devon.

Before moving to No 5 Oakhill, he lived in Hesle House in Epsom Road, Ewell.

The clergyman's neighbours in the mid-1930s included Leonard Underwood at No 6, and flat-dwellers Edward Godden, Duncan Cameron, Mrs Powers, Gilbert Bryant and Thomas Pollard in No 7.

At the time No 9 Oakhill was the Oakenshaw Private Hotel, kept by Theobald Cocquerel.

Early in the year 2004, No 3 Oakhill was still standing but was quite run down and had been the Newlands Nurses Home Project Department, at the rear of which was the modern Oakhill Health Centre. There was no longer a number 4 but Nos 5 and 6 were the original villas, now flats. No 6 bears the original name Crown Lodge.

Kingswood Close was constructed alongside No 6 before 1970.

Children's author Christine Wood wrote many of her books at her home in the modern end of Oak Hill during the 1970s and 1980s.

Although she is known primarily for her children's books, which carry a Christian message, before her allegiance to Baptist and Evangelical Churches, she was a member of the exclusive Plymouth Brethren. A biographical account of her days with the Brethren was published in the 1970s and raised more than a few eyebrows. She also contributed to the Guide Post magazines.

Mrs Wood's first husband died after dental surgery and she remarried. Her second husband was Douglas Wood, so she had no need to change her name. Christine and Douglas worshipped at Surbiton Baptist Church, Balaclava Road, for many years but in recent years attended services at Hook Evangelical Church, Brook Road, Hook.

The Oak Hill properties date back to the 1850s. They took a long time to construct and in some cases, money ran out before they could be completed. The Oak Hill area was drained in 1865 after which the roads on the estate became less caked in mud.

Originally, Oak Hill, Oak Hill Road and Oak Hill Grove were known as The Parade. This title was later only applied to Oak Hill, beginning with Elmside at the far end near Oakhill Path and going as far as a property known as Mona Lodge.

Mona Lodge was once the home of Archdeacon Philpott. Later in the Victorian era, it was the residence of Charles Walpole.

Mr Walpole was a prominent Surbiton figure who was a key member of the Surbiton Improvement Commissioners.

This board was formed in 1855 following an act of Parliament.

No 3 Oakhill in 2004.

Elmside No 1 Oakhill formerly a Surbiton Hospital nurses' home.

Inverbrae, No 2 Oakhill — still standing proud in the year 2004.

No 5 Oakhill at the start of the 21st century. A typical mid-Victorian Surbiton villa.

The Sanctuary (formerly Mountcoombe Hotel) in present times.

Crown Lodge — No 6 Oakhill.

Ardmay Hotel, Avenue Elmers

Charles Walpole lived at Mona Lodge, Oak Hill, until he moved to Chobham in 1874. He had been chairman of the Surbiton Improvement Commissioners' Board.

Mr Walpole

CHARLES Walpole was a prominent Surbiton resident who was a key member of the Surbiton Commissioners. This board was formed in 1855 after the passing of a Bill in Parliament which gave Surbiton self-controlled local government. Kingston had unsuccessfully tried to "take" Surbiton for itself the previous year but Surbiton ratepayers had staged an uprising over the plans.

THE ARDMAY HOTEL
SURBITON

This was the heyday of The Ardmay Hotel, in Avenue Elmers, Surbiton. Here, in the 1930s, double rooms could be rented for five shillings and sixpence (27p) a week or six shillings (30p) for a single room. All mattresses were sprung and an added attraction was hot and and cold water in each room. The hotel site, next to the former Romanoff School, was redeveloped as Ardmay Gardens in 1958.

Old cars filled with concrete were designed to act as defences against a German invasion on the Kingston bypass at Tolworth in the Second World War. A pillbox-type structure appears to have been constructed on the roundabout along with other hastily-built fortifications aimed at impeding the progress of any tanks arriving outside the Odeon cinema — now the site of Tolworth Tower.

Rylands, Hudson's and Packham's
Recalling Surbiton shops

Born in the 1920s, Joyce Eggleton grew up at a time when there were many family-owned shops in Surbiton. Shopping was an adventure for a young child in the pre-Second World War days.

In retirement at New Malden, Joyce (Gardner) looked back affectionately at some of Surbiton's stores.

Rylands, (Joseph Edgar Ryland, draper, No 27 Victoria Road). "It was a big ladies' shop. It sold petticoats, pinafores, underwear, paint jackets and white trousers to wear when painting and decorating. Things went along on wire pulleys, making a clicking sound, and the shop assistant would send the change back on it."

"**Lowe,** the chemist, on the corner of Claremont Road and St Mark's Hill, had large red, yellow, and blue bottles on the shelves."

Sainsbury's (Nos 2 & 3 Victoria Road — in modern times Martin's newsagent's and post office) "was not much more than a couple of counters".

Hudson's (No 12 Victoria Road, provision merchant's and grocer's) was similar in style to Sainsbury's with food counters. "It was quite old-fashioned and sold good quality food. I remember one walkway up the middle of the shop."

Packham's (H. Packham & Sons Ltd, 8 Victoria Road — bakers and wine & spirit merchants) "was a high-class baker's. They used to cater for wedding receptions.

"If they had any cakes left over at the end of the day, you could buy them next morning. Fourteen for a penny."

Bull's (Bull and Son, stationers and printers, bookbinders and booksellers, 20 Victoria Road) was "quite an old-fashioned lovely shop where they ordered any book you wanted."

Timothy White's (No 45d Victoria Road, domestic stores, established 1928) "had an upstairs and

Victoria Road, Surbiton, in the mid-1930s.

downstairs. You could get anything you wanted from Timothy White's — kitchenware, bathroom items, you name it. It was a wonderful shop and we were very sad when it eventually closed."

Mac Fisheries (No 61 Brighton Road before relocating to Victoria Road) was next door-but-one to the corner of Brighton Road and Balaclava Road. Right on the corner was Arthur Millen, the butcher's shop, in later years, a corn merchant, then a garden supplies shop and much more recently a fish restaurant with a finely restored clock tower above.

Two **Co-op** stores traded in Brighton Road on opposite sides of the street — at No 55 and at Nos 44-48. The Royal Arsenal Co-operative Society at No 55 sold only clothes; the other side groceries.

"Customers were handed tokens according to how much they spent and you collected these. My mother had thousands. Then you could exchange them for Co-op dividends."

Jordan's (toy dealers, No 28 Victoria Road). "We used to call this place 'the dolls' hospital'. It was a beautiful toy shop and I used to go in there when I was five years old. The man who ran

it was very nice. You could take your doll there to have a new wig. The dolls lay in cots waiting to be treated. It was like a dolls' hospital. In recent times it was a hairdresser's."

Unigate Dairy was on the corner of Brighton Road and Victoria Avenue. (In modern times, it has traded as the Kentucky Fried Chicken outlet). "I remember that a Miss Nelson and her elderly mother lived above and they had windows which curved round towards Victoria Avenue. Miss Nelson was sometimes employed by the BBC as a whistler. She whistled on certain programmes they were making and was quite skilled at it." Next door to Unigate was **Lamdin's,** the bootmaker's.

Brighton Road (Electric Parade) a century ago.

Joyce Eggleton.

'Is there really a place called Surbiton?'
The Good Life myth

People living in other parts of the country are sometimes heard to comment: "Is there really a place called Surbiton?" and "I thought it was a made-up name for television". Their curiosity was aroused after watching a new BBC situation comedy concerning self-sufficiency in suburbia.

A total of 30 episodes ran for four years centred upon a special slice of Surbiton life in The Avenue, and 'The Good Life' has enjoyed repeated showings on TV ever since as one of the classic comedies of all time.

Tom Good, played by Richard Briers, had reached his 40th birthday and become weary of the rat race. Each day he would commute to his draughtsman's job in the City, where he designed plastic toys for cereal packets for the JJM company.

Tom found it all too mundane and decided to throw it all in and focus on farming — at home.

His wife Barbara (Felicity Kendal) provided much assistance, and ideas. Together they turned the front and back gardens into an allotment for fruit, vegetables and livestock.

The next-door neighbours, Margo and Jerry Leadbetter (Penelope Keith and Paul Eddington) expressed their disap-

The Good Life actors — from left to right Felicity Kendal and Richard Briers, who played Barbara and Tom; and Paul Eddington and Penelope Keith remembered by many for their roles as Jerry and Margo Leadbetter.

This advertisement for The Good Life bistro, Surbiton, appeared in the Surrey Comet in 1984.

pointment and pomposity on a grand scale after waking each morning to the sound of pigs and hens, not forgetting Lenin the cockerel and Geraldine the goat.

The Goods obtained their heating and warmth from an old cast-iron range — quite a fashionable kitchen item in years to come — and for electricity they ran a generator in the cellar. Any home-grown produce surplus to requirements would be bartered with the local shopkeepers.

Creators and writers, John Esmonde and Bob Larbey, considered Surbiton to be the ideal suburban setting and the search started for two suitable houses side by side. They were found in "The Avenue" — one slightly run-down in 1930s' style and the other immaculate, with bay windows and a much smarter garden.

Richard Briers had appeared in 'Brothers In Law' and 'Marriage Lines' as well as numerous other comedy roles, but

it was The Good Life that really made him a household name. It was also a great help in making his co-stars famous, although they had done much TV and theatre work previously.

Paul Eddington appeared as Will Scarlett in the 1950s' TV show 'The Adventures of Robin Hood' made at Walton Studios, just a few miles from Surbiton.

Life in the Good garden was not easy. Jerry and Margo had decided that their neighbours were completely insane but they became loyal friends.

Jerry, who had been a former work colleague of Tom's, took a lot of interest in developments next door, and he and Margo, who hated wellies, even helped out in times of crisis.

The Leadbetters, who were wealthier and often snobbish in outlook, were rewarded with the Good's positive, wholesale and cheerful attitude.

Margo's character filled out as the show progressed and if

Surbiton was regarded as the Queen of the Suburbs, then Margo Leadbetter, with her snooty and domineering manner, was surely the Empress of Suburbia.

In the 1970s, the idea of alternative lifestyle was very much in vogue and the programme had a remarkable effect. Thousands of people decided to start growing their own produce. Lawns were dug up, vegetables pushed aside the flowers, and goat–keeping was on the increase.

By 1980, there was a record number of 51,000 smallholdings in Britain.

Tom and Barbara lived at No 55 The Avenue and for filming, the real owners agreed to have their front and back lawns dug up, then covered in vegetables with some animals running around for good measure.

One of the rooms in the house was also used as a costume and make-up store.

At the end of the series, the BBC crew would dig up all the crops and turf the garden over, and the whole exercise would be repeated for two more series.

The team even built a patio for the real occupants at the end of the last series as a thank-you gesture.

One memorable episode involved the fire brigade standing in the front garden, aiming their hoses over the roof into the back garden to simulate heavy rain. The resulting muddy vegetable plots proved to be too slippery for Margo's wellies.

A Christmas special was made in 1977 called 'Silly But It's Fun', when all four drank pea-pod wine and wore newspaper hats. The following year, The Queen was asked to help raise money for British athletes competing in the Commonwealth Games. This she did by picking a TV programme she would like to see being made, with a specially invited audience. She chose The Good Life and this last show entitled 'When I'm 65' was completed on 10th June 1978.

'Surbiton Common' — in reality long-since disappeared — Thames Ditton and Esher, all got a mention in the programme.

The actual house used for the filming increased in value and the real owners moved out when the final series ended.

So where was 'The Avenue'? Its namesake can be found in the Berrylands area. But that's not the one.

Surbiton locations were considered for the series but none of the residents were happy to see their gardens change beyond all recognition.

In the end two suitable houses were found in Kewferry Road, Northwood, Middlesex, but they did look as if they belonged to Surbiton.

At least the 'Good' house at No 55 produced very good plants for years to come, thanks to it being dug over and manured so much.

In 2002-3, Penelope Keith was seen at many functions around Surrey when she held the position of High Sheriff of Surrey.

The High Sheriff's role is traditionally one of representing the Queen. In some people's eyes, perhaps, she was representing the Queen of the Suburbs.

The Good Life restaurant, No 3 Central Parade, St Mark's Hill, pictured in March 2004.

The Good Life bistro

The Good Life Bistro opened in Central Parade, St Mark's Hill, in 1980 preserving the name of the well-known television programme.

The fully licensed venue, managed by Alistair and Vicky Spence, offered "intimate friendly atmosphere combined with excellent food and wine at a price everyone can afford".

It was very popular with the locals and even offered a traditional Sunday roast.

In modern times, the bistro traded as a fish and chip outlet but the name was kept.

The Salad Bowl

The Salad Bowl Restaurant at No 9 Claremont Road was renowned for its salads and ice cream melbas according to this 1948 advertisement.

World flight record in 1926

The widow of one of the world's most courageous pioneer aviators lived for more than 30 years in Surbiton. But this little-known fact only came to light recently when a mystery batch of black and white photographs were discovered in an attic.

Bernie Deadman, who runs the Maypole Guest House at No 18 Hook Road, Surbiton, with his wife, Mary, had found the large military pictures when he went into the loft in 1986 to tinker with a troublesome tank and nearly tripped over a timber trunk with rope handles.

Inside the old chest were five large prints showing two smart young airmen and their uniformed colleagues. The pictures appeared to have been taken at the RAF training college in Cranwell.

Sixteen years later, Mrs Deadman asked Mark Davison, who at the time was researching his book, Hook Remembered Again, if he could investigate further in the hope that the family photos could be returned to their rightful owners.

In one of the picture's captions, one of the airmen was listed as being T. Neville Stack. The name Stack was also on a badge sewn on one of the young men's shirts in another picture. In addition, the photos were wrapped up in brown paper, on which had been written: "Mrs T. Neville Stack, The Mountcoombe Hotel, Surbiton," along with an Elmbridge (Surbiton) exchange telephone number.

Searches of electoral registers and Kelly's directories revealed that a Mrs Edythe Neville Stack lived at No 18 Hook Road from the early 1950s until her death in 1984. That year, it was later learnt, she died soon after a road accident while she was crossing Hook Road on a shopping trip.

An entry in Who's Who showed that Mrs Neville Stack (better known as "Tizza") was the widow of pioneer aviator Captain Thomas Neville Stack. Furthermore her son, also Thomas, was a noted airman as well who rose to the ranks of Air Chief Marshall and became deputy captain of the Queen's Flight and was also Her Majesty's gentleman usher for 11 years from 1979 to 1989.

A love of flying ran in the family, it became clear. Tizza's husband joined the Royal Engineers in 1914 and was a motor-

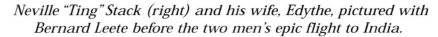
Neville "Ting" Stack (right) and his wife, Edythe, pictured with Bernard Leete before the two men's epic flight to India.

Neville "Ting" Stack — first to fly to India from the UK in a light aircraft.

cycle despatch rider. He served in France for two years in the First World War, serving as a corporal with the 8th Division (23rd Infantry Brigade).

He was commissioned in June 1917 and became an instructor in flying and air navigation while being a flight commander and acting captain of the 121 Squadron.

From 1919-1921 he held the position as chief pilot and instructor of the London and Provincial Aviation Company, during which time he was in charge of the flying organisation concerned with the delivery of newspapers such as the Daily Sketch and Evening Standard by air for the Hulton Press.

The sky was the limit for young Neville Stack who became known affectionately as "Ting". From 1921 to 1925, he

rejoined the RAF and was employed as an instructor on multi-engined aircraft and served three years in Iraq with No 70 Bomber and Transport Squadron. During this period, he was engaged in operations in Kurdistan — bombing, troop transportation and air mail between Cairo and Baghdad.

Ting, who was born in April 1896, relinquished his commission and became chief instructor to the Lancashire Aero Club from 1925 to 1927. It was during this time he made a world record flight to India in a Moth light aircraft.

On a cold, murky and blustery 16th November 1926, Ting climbed into a single-seater De Havilland Moth, powered by a Cirrus Mk II engine with the ambition of becoming the first person to fly a light aircraft to India.

He was accompanied in a similar Moth by pilot Bernard Leete. The two took off from Stag Lane Aerodrome and flew to Lympne airfield, Kent, for customs clearance before their epic journey.

His wife, wrapped up against the cold and threatening rain, and wearing a flower-pot hat and a fur collar, was at Stag Lane to bid the two men farewell.

Ting later recalled: "The engines started with that wonderful promptitude for which the Cirrus (engine) is so renowned and ticked over beautifully. We said cheerio to our relatives and friends, acknowledged the plaudits of the crowd, who cheered both of us, and we were away. By the time we reached Lympne, it was blowing half a gale which made things somewhat awkward for landing. Luckily Commander Deacon and his very efficient staff were waiting for us and managed to grasp our wing-tips immediately we had landed, otherwise, in our light little machines, we might easily have been blown right over."

He continued: "Commander Deacon was most hospitable, and among other kindnesses, brewed us his special and delicious coffee. He was a father to us and would not let us budge for three and a half days."

On 20th November, the two men set off for Paris. The trip was a little bumpy and the rainclouds made the flight over hills difficult. They landed at Le Bourget and were greeted by Jimmy Youell, of Imperial Airways. Gales held them up for two days and then they climbed again into the skies, later landing at Lyons without lights or flares. The airfield's equipment had been damaged in the previous day's gales.

After two more days of bad weather, forcing a delay, the adventurers flew down the Rhone Valley between the mountains to Marseille. Next day, they passed Nice, Monaco, Mentone and Genoa en route to Pisa where the aerodrome was flooded and landing was hazardous. The Italian air force welcomed the men.

Next day, the pair left for Rome where they visited the historical city. Poor weather again enforced hold-ups. On the last day of November they pushed on to Sicily and Malta, skirting Mount Vesuvius and commenting they were like "moths round a flame". They also saw the smoking snow-capped Mount Etna, before landing at Catania in Sicily. In Malta they received cherished hospitality from the Governor, Sir Roger Keyes, and Lady Congreve, for seven days until storms passed.

On 8th December, they crossed the Mediterranean and reached Tripoli. "The sea crossing seemed to take centuries and there was no shipping in sight." They were again greeted

Neville "Ting" Stack — made headlines in the 1920s and 1930s with his record flights in light aircraft, just years after accomplishments of a similar nature by Harry Hawker, of Hook Road. Stack's wife lived for 30 years in Hook Road — just a mile from Hawker.

heartily by Italians. Next day they were bound for Benghazi, a trip of some 450 miles, which included flying over the hostile Libyan Desert. The journey took six hours and there was inclement weather. At Benghazi, they were welcomed by British Consul and Commandante Sala, air officer in command at Benghazi who told the pilots he would "be their mother-in-law" during their stay.

They set off in thunder and rain for Porto Bardia and after more than four hours' flying were "nearly blown over" on landing. On December 12th, they left for Cairo, completing the 400-mile trip in four hours and 50 minutes.

"We were given a grand time and a wonderful welcome had been arranged for us by Flight Lieutenant "Taffy " Jones. Everyone showed great interest in the flight and the little

Moth machines that carried us so far over land and sea."

On the 14th, they departed for Baghdad. The trip was broken into three stages on account of strong contrary winds. They passed over the Suez Canal, through Palestine and over the Judean hills and Dead Sea, "leaving Jerusalem on our left and thence to Ziza in Transjordania."

One of Leete's magnetos had failed as they prepared to leave Amman after an overnight stay. But undeterred, they crossed the desert with only one functioning on his engine. After a night at Rutbah Wells, they continued on to Baghdad the next morning.

A wonderful welcome was given to the delighted men on their arrival at Baghdad by Squadrons 70 and 55. "People were amazed at and full of praise for the two small Moth machines that had crossed the famous desert air mail track unescorted," Stack chronicled.

On Christmas Eve 1926, the men continued their journey to Basra. The magneto had been repaired at Baghdad.

They spent Christmas Day and Boxing Day with 84 Squadron at Shiba. Ting has blurred memories of the 25th on account of the celebratory drinking but remembers saying the wrong things to inebriated navy personnel disguised in air men's uniforms and vice versa.

Later on Boxing Day they were up in the air again, passing the great oil port of the Anglo-Persian Oil Company at Abbadan and the swamps in the Persian Gulf. A difficult landing had to be made on a very narrow strip owing to oily plugs.

Soon, the pair were on the last leg of their voyage to India, but not before Ting discovered a cracked cylinder head which had to be repaired with Hermatite. They had stopped at Bushire and met Air Minister Sir Samuel Hoare, in his De Havilland 66.

"It was very pleasant meeting this party in such a remote spot."

More cylinder head problems bedevilled the last leg of the flight, as well as choking dust storms which meant they could not see the ground. Eventually, in triumphant style, they touched down in India after a journey described by the editor of Airways magazine as "the finest light aeroplane achievement in the history of British aviation."

The Indian flight was not Neville Stack's only flying achievement. In 1927, he flew the first scheduled light aeroplane flight of 5,000 miles through France, Spain, North Africa and Italy.

The following year, he achieved the light aerodrome record flight from London to Berlin in four hours and 50 minutes.

In 1929, he succeeded in completing a 6,000-mile demonstration tour for S. Smith and Sons.

In 1930, he flew from London to Baghdad, a distance of 2,550 miles, in 32 hours. And that year, he also piloted the first demonstration tour of Europe in a Loncock single-seater fighter for the Blackburn Aircraft Company.

Then, in 1931, he flew from Zlín, Czechoslovakia, to Calcutta and back to Zlín with Tomáš Bata, of the famous Bata shoe firm, piloting a three-engined Fokker.

The next year he flew from Blackpool to Karachi in a Spartan mail plane and in 1933, he went from London to Bombay and back. It was a mercy mission with a surgeon to operate on the Maharanee of Nepal.

Ting, who died in about 1949, will also go down in history for other record flights. In 1930, he flew from London to Berlin and back — a trip of 1,200 miles — in nine hours and 30 minutes. The same year, he achieved London to Copenhagen and back in nine hours and 50 minutes, and a return trip to Constantinople (now Istanbul) in 12 hours. This was a journey of 1,750 miles.

On top of this, he could boast of smashing another record:

Neville "Ting" Stack after receiving the Air Force Cross from King George V in 1927 for his world-record flight to India in a light aircraft.

Wife of a famous pilot: Edythe "Tizza" Neville Stack, who lived in No 18 Hook Road, Surbiton, for more than 30 years.

London to Warsaw and back (2,000 miles) in just 17 hours.

Mr and Mrs Neville Stack had two sons, Thomas (known as Jimmy) and Anthony and grandchildren Janice, Carolyn, Andrew and Georgina. It was "Jimmy" Neville Stack, who served the Queen and became an air chief marshall. Anthony chose not to pursue a career in the air force.

Thomas "Jimmy" Neville Stack pictured in 1939 and as Air Chief Marshal during his time serving the Queen. He was the son of the air pioneer Thomas Neville "Ting" Stack.

In July 1939, Neville "Ting"Stack's flying career nearly came to a tragic end when a plane crashed on a test flight while he worked for a Midlands aircraft factory. His legs were broken in eight places. One leg was in plaster of Paris for eight months and it wasn't until March 1941 that he was fit enough to have his 'B' licence returned to him by the Air Ministry. Then, once again, there was no stopping him. Three days after the accident, Neville Stack's son, Jimmy, was awarded the Sword of Honour at RAF Cranwell.

Mrs Neville Stack's home in Hook Road, built in 1902, started life as Derrynane. It was built on meadowland which belonged to Malvern Lodge, over the road. Malvern Lodge was demolished in the early 1930s and Malvern Court flats built on the site.

Opposite her home stood Holmbury, where in 1874, author Thomas Hardy lived with his wife Emma following their wedding. Holly trees which until recently had grown outside Derrynane are thought to have featured in one of Hardy's poems from that period.

No 18 was bought by Bernie and Mary Deadman in 1986 from a dentist, Dr Roberts, who specialised in cleft palates and worked closely with Guy's Hospital. Mr and Mrs Deadman had run the Duke of Buckingham public house, Villiers Road, Kingston, for seven years from 1979. Before that, they

Mrs Mary Deadman, in February 2004, outside No 18 Hook Road, the former home of Mrs Neville Stack. Mrs Deadman opened the Maypole Guest House here in 1986.

had kept The Pilot pub, in a "hard" part of Deptford. Bernie was in the London Fire Brigade for 17 years before that, mainly stationed at Kensington. Mary was a secretary for C.F Anderson, a large timber firm in Islington. She hails from Cork, Ireland, and came to England in 1950 when she was nine. Bernie's father was a boatbuilder in Enfield, Middlesex.

Mrs Neville Stack moved into No 18 Hook Road after living in rooms at The Mountcoombe Hotel, Oak Hill, Surbiton, following the death of her pilot husband. The house was bought for her by her son, Thomas (Jimmy).

Newspaper headlines from 1941 told of Neville Stack senior's return to flying.

Jimmy had a distinguished career. Between 1973 and 1975, he was an air officer commanding the RAF Training College, Cranwell. He was aide-de-camp to the Queen from 1976-78 and director general of the Asbestos International Association, 1978-1979. He was a Freeman of the City of London, a liveryman, and Air Secretary, 1976-78. He was awarded the CBE, CVO, CB, KCB and Air Force Cross.

After his death in the early 1990s, his wife, Lady Stack, continued to reside at their marital home in a smart part of Fulham. Mrs Stack often used to visit Hook Road with her husband. Towards the end, she said, her mother-in-law sadly allowed the house to get into a state of disrepair.

She said that Mrs Neville Stack's mother, a Mrs Lyster, also lived at the address and received a telegram from the Queen when she reached 100 years of age.

A postcard from Surbiton Hill Park, 1942

SURBITON HILL PARK.

A.S. 5205.

This is how Surbiton Hill Park, Berrylands, looked during the Second World War. The view is from a post-card sent by a Katie Partridge to her parents at Leigh-on-Sea, Essex, on 2nd February 1942. In fountain pen ink, she writes: "Dear Mum. Arrived here quite safely without any mishap. It was snowing all the way and today it has got to the slushy stage. Hope Dad got home safely. Also hope you didn't have any more alarms. Love from Kate." These houses, built on farmland in the early 1930s, were then quite new.

Ken Armstrong gives a few tips to a young Surrey fan.

Ken Armstrong

A TOP footballer who played for England and Chelsea in the mid 1950s, lived at No 7 Pembroke Avenue, off Surbiton Hill Park in 1955.

The late Ken Armstrong was a legend in the game. His transfer from Bradford Rovers to Chelsea was said to have been the greatest bargain of all time in the football world. The fee was 100 guineas. He was Chelsea captain, appearing a record 474 times for the club and leading them to their only championship in 1955. He starred in a famous 7-2 England victory over Scotland at Wembley in 1955 before moving to New Zealand in 1957 and continuing his noteworthy career, even playing in a major team at the age of 45.

Winnie, 90, looks back on "dear little Surbiton" and Tolworth

WINNIE Randall moved to Cleaveland Road, Surbiton, six months after she was born in April 1913 at Southfields, London. Her elder brother Jack was born two years later. At the age of 90, Winnie often looked back fondly on her girlhood days.

"My mother always took me shopping in Victoria Road. There was a plaster dog, like a terrier, sat in the corner of a leather shop, on the left-hand side going towards the post office. I would never let Mum go anywhere without first letting me see this 'Bow Wow' as I called it. I wonder what happened to it and the leather shop?

"We moved to Worthington Road, Tolworth, later, but always visited Surbiton, a dear, select little town — my favourite.

"Tolworth had some nice shops, too, even during the First World War. There used to be a big one called Cliffords *(Clifford, Sons and Co. Ltd, 268-270 Ewell Road, grocers and post office, between Ditton Road and Worthington Road).*

"Cliffords had a wine and spirits entrance as you went towards the back of the shop and opposite there was a grocery department with glass-topped biscuit tins over the counter which contained gorgeous chocolate biscuits with crystallised violets and roses on top. They were so much more delicious than today's biscuits.

"There was also a little red post box with the posting times outside.

"A young man who worked at the provisions counter in Clifford's had an impediment in his speech. Instead of saying 1/6d, he would say 'one and shix'. He really got teased. Us girls often went in just to see the fun.

"One day one boy kept teasing him until he was really upset. He lunged at him with a sharp knife shouting from the counter: 'You little b----r' until the boy was really upset.

"This boy ran like mad not looking where he was going. There were two wooden boxes filled with cheap cracked eggs, a penny and three-farthings a dozen for cooking. These boxes were stood balanced, one on top of the other, outside the shop. Well, this young fellow ran in his fright right into these two boxes and you can imagine the state he was in.

"There was a song that ran: 'I fell in a box of eggs and all the yellow ran down my legs, when I fell in a box of eggs.' We used to sing it to him and he got mad.

Ewell Road, near Worthington Road. Clifford's store is on the right. Inset: Winnie Randall in 1917.

"Two very nice ladies worked on the grocery side of Clifford's and wore black sateen aprons. They were Miss Godwin and Miss Salter. Rose Salter lived in Worthington Road. They always said: 'Yes, Winnie?' when I went in. Mum always dealt in Clifford's rather than Eccles up the road.

"Mother was very sharp to me. She loved boys best. She used to say: 'I wish I had had all boys'. When I was very young I thought you could choose. I replied: 'Why didn't you then?' Then I got a slap.

"Well, one day, Mum was having a friend to tea, so she said to me: 'Run down the road and get 1lb of best mixed biscuits and don't be long'. She always said 'Don't be all day', which worried me. I was frightened of mother. So off I went into Clifford's

shop and either Miss Godwin or Miss Salter asked: 'Yes, Winnie?'. Oh dear, I had clean forgotten Mum's order. Then, in my fright, I stammered out: 'messed bix miskits'. The assistant said: 'Oh we don't keep those'. I felt shocked. Then she said, 'You mean best mixed biscuits?' Oh, the relief. I replied: 'Yes please'.

"I rushed back and Mum said: "What a time you've been and grabbed the packet. I ran off so relieved I had got her order right and expected a good wallop.

"When you went into Clifford's, on the left hand side was a door and inside a telephone with a sign which read: 'You may telephone from here'. A telephone! It was so different from the ones of today. You lifted the phone off the hook at the side to phone. The Post Office was at the end of the shop with a big wire screen over the top. There was no protection like those of today to stop crooks and robbers.

"The stamps for letters were red and cost three-halfpence. Halfpenny stamps for postcards were green.

"Oh, the jolly times and tunes in the roaring twenties.

"Next door to Cliffords there was a classy butcher's, called Stevens, in modern times a cycle shop.

"You can still see the hooks where the joints of meat were hung. Now cycles hang up there.

"Further along there was another grocery provisions shop, called H.P. Eccles *(284 Ewell Road)*. My dad used to laugh and say 'H. Peccles', putting the 'p' on Eccles.

"Opposite was my school, St Matthew's Girls' Church School *(which became Surbiton Police Station)*. I went there from 1919 to 1927. Miss Passey was the first teacher I knew when I left the lower classes. When she knew about the boy falling into the boxes of eggs, Miss Passey said: 'Serves him very well right', instead of 'jolly well right'. She always said: 'Very well'. My father, who was a bit of a joker, thought it very funny and always mimicked her by saying: 'Very well right'.

"Winnie's mother, Edna, died of stomach cancer in November 1927 in the family flat at No 34 Worthington Road and in 1932 the family moved to Buckinghamshire.

"We had enjoyed a lot of jolly times in Tolworth and had lots of playmates in the 1920s.

"There was lovely countryside beyond the Red Lion public house. No Broadway then. There was a lovely walk up a shady lane to Old Malden fields. One could pick big flowers called dog daisies and a bigger type called horse daisies. When you got to the top, there was a stile and fields where you could hear the bells of St John's Church pealing so sweetly on a Sunday. There were poppies and giant scabious flowering in the tall grass. There was a white wooden bridge and a stream in which we played as children in the school holidays. Ah! These were sweet, happy days, so different to now.

"I had two friends at school, sisters Ethel and Eleanor Spencer, whose family ran the Victoria Inn on Surbiton Hill *(No 143 Ewell Road, kept by Edward Beckwith Spencer)*. Ethel wanted to be an actress and Eleanor had lovely auburn hair. I worshipped those two girls. They were older than myself. I often wondered what happened to those two girls. I also wish I knew what happened to Miss Raleigh, a teacher at school. She lived in Cotterill Road and rode a squeaky bike to school and back. She had a son called Tony and was a First World War widow.

Wirth's shop can be seen to the rear of Tolworth fountain, in this Edwardian photograph. The fountain stood proudly in the Ewell Road, near the junction of Ditton Road from 1901 until its removal was deemed necessary in 1936 owing to a huge increase in traffic.

Shopkeeper 'who never washed'

On the corner of Beaconsfield Road and Ewell Road in the 1920s was a higgledy-piggledy shop called Wirth's. The state of the shop became the subject of gossip among customers and local residents.

Winnie Randall recalled: "The shop was run by a German called Herman Wirth. It sold everything from gas mantles and small screws to jam and plants.

"Mrs Wirth was a homely old lady. They had been there years and years.

"One day Mr Wirth was taken to hospital with pneumonia and he soon after died. The tale went round that when they washed him in hospital he died because they had cleaned the dirt off his body and that gave him a chill. He had never washed, so the story went. His shop was always jumbled up, but they were friendly, helpful people.

"Also in Beaconsfield Road was a bicycle hire business run by the Lale family. They charged sixpence for half an hour's hire and a shilling for an hour."

Sweetshop man in a fluster over dolly mixtures

Ewell Road, Surbiton, in the 1930s. The Prince of Wales inn is on the right, opposite Farmers, the butcher's and poulterer's.

Some of the shops on Surbiton Hill in the 1930s. On the far right is F&C White, fancy draper, 114 Ewell Road.

LIFE in Surbiton and Tolworth during the 1920s was quite different to today's. There was no television, very few had telephones, and there was little traffic on the roads. Trams ran through both areas and there was generally a semi-rural feel about the locality.

Winnie Randall lived as a girl in Worthington Road, Tolworth, and at the age of 90 was able to look back fondly on the days of her youth.

She had a wealth of anecdotes from the past which she loved sharing with others.

"There were some lovely shops at the top of Surbiton Hill, going up from Tolworth. Pearks *(Pearks Dairy Ltd, grocers, No 150 Ewell Road next to R Thirlby and Son, dairy)* was one. And there was a lovely big shop called Jamesons, similar to the Cliffords shop in Tolworth. They used to sell broken biscuits. Us children loved to go and buy some. There was quite a variety and some biscuits were not broken at all. Sadly the shop is now a posh restaurant. Another shop we went in was the Home and Colonial Stores *(No 161 Ewell Road six doors up from the junction with Browns Road).*

W.E.Clarke, chemist *(No 169 Ewell Road, on the corner of Browns Road and established in 1893)* is also recalled by Winnie and she was delighted that it survived until the turn of the 21st Century.

"The sweet shop next to the chemist was owned by an old man called Mr Thomas. He had an impediment in his speech and always sounded as if he was grunting. He always wore a tweed hat.

"My young brother, Victor, loved dolly mixtures — small sweets for young children. He was three years old when Mum took him in for some. My older brother, Jack, and myself stayed outside. We watched Vic say to Mr Thomas: 'Dolly Mixture, please' and pointed to the jar. Mr Thomas looked and said: 'Arpine Micture?' Vic replied, almost crying: 'No, no!'. By this time, Jack and I were in fits of laughter outside. Mr Thomas saw us and swore. He also shook his fist at us. My mother said they were her son and daughter. At last Dolly Mixtures were weighed out and Mr Thomas said: 'Why didn't you say Dolly Mixture?' Mum and Vic came out very happy and relieved.

"When Dad heard about it, he always called Dolly Mixtures Arpine Mictures. We never went into that shop again.

"Further down the road was a shoe repairer called Russell. *(Mr Frank Russell, boot maker, No 149 Ewell Road, Surbiton Hill).* I was always frightened of him. He had a lot of clattering machines overhead and wore a dirty brown overall. He also had a very red face.

"We used to take our repairs to my friend's father, Percy Bailey, who was a first class repairer. Oh the twenties! Clattering trams. How they used to clatter down Surbiton Hill and and pull up outside the Royal Oak pub. We could hear them in the night.

"One day, when my brother Jack was about two or three years old, he was sitting in a high chair at home in Worthington Road eating a pink blancmange mother had made when all of a sudden he upped the plate and clapped it on top of his head, blancmange and all. I can see him now. Mum said his hair had a pink tinge long after.

"In the twenties, blancmange powders contained extracts of real fruit, so the colours were strong.

"At school, our teacher Miss Passey asked us to take turns reading out of a book. One girl misread the word pyjamas as 'pie james'. Miss Passey said: 'Good gracious. What are you saying and told her what it should have said. How we laughed. I also remember some of the other teachers — Miss Schofield, Miss Tranter and Miss Molly Peck. I left St Matthew's School in 1926.

"Around this time, there were wind-up gramophones with a black bottom. It cost seven shillings and sixpence for a double spring, three shillings and sixpence for a single spring. When the spring broke, it made an awful clonk and the record gradually slowed down."

St George's Church, Tolworth

A procession of witness was held along the Ewell Road in 1959 to mark the 25th anniversary of St George's Church, Hamilton Avenue, Tolworth. The congregation members paraded from St George's to St Matthew's Church. The front two ladies are (kerbside) Mrs Maisie Collins and (offside), Pat "Binkie" Piper, a teacher trained at Whitelands College, Putney. Behind her is Eileen Stone, also a teacher trained at the same college. Eileen some years later moved to Bungay, Suffolk.

Having tonsils out

SURBITON Cottage Hospital opened in St James' Road in 1883 and elderly pensioners can still remember being treated there in the 1920s before the main Surbiton Hospital was built at Ewell Road, Surbiton Hill, in 1936.

Winnie Randall at the age of 91 looked back on the day she had her tonsils out at the cottage hospital.

"Two nurses took our hands and slid us along the polished floor to the operating theatre. It was such fun — until the ether mask was slapped on our face. We also had to wear long woollen stockings, a long gown and a rubber cap in which our hair was gathered. The mask made you fuzzy in the head. A strict nurse said to me: 'You dare be sick, my girl.' I woke up surrounded by a lot of enamel dishes full of blood."

Jimmy White

SNOOKER supremo Jimmy White lived at Middlecot, No 10 Hook Road in the late 1990s.

After a family break-up he moved to Oxshott. His wife believed the house was haunted by the ghosts of clergymen who resided there decades ago.

Thomas Hardy

AUTHOR Thomas Hardy lived at No 13 Hook Road – now Midhurst Court flats – in 1874-5 with his wife Emma after they honeymooned in Paris. It was at Hook Road, while sharing a house with Mr and Mrs William David Hughes and their daughter Annie, (born 1868; pictured) that he began his major novel, The Hand of Ethelberta.

Annie Hughes.

Surbiton's link with Bryant and May matches

Inside the kitchen area of Hillcroft College (formerly The Gables) in the early 1930s.

Hillcroft College, South Bank, Surbiton, just before the Second World War.   *Wilberforce Bryant.*

SURBITON can claim fame to having as one of its past important residents a key member of the Bryant and May matches firm.

Wilberforce Bryant, who was chairman of the company, was extremely wealthy. His family held the British patent for safety matches.

The town attracted many well-off businessmen after they had made their money. Bryant was one of them. At the age of 40, he had a large house, The Gables, built at South Bank, Surbiton, in 1877. In 1926, long after the Bryants had departed, the house became Hillcroft College. The house was designed so that the servants' quarters were kept apart from the main building.

The Bryant family were Quakers and Wilberforce was a community-minded man who was quick to dig deep into his pocket to help worthy causes in Surbiton.

He sponsored two coffee taverns, The Spread Eagle and The Anchor in the town. Moreover, he also had built in 1884 The Gables Theatre, erected on the site of Bath Lodge in the grounds of his mansion. Although it was felt the theatre had been put up as a "folly" for the owner, it was soon beloved by amateur theatrical companies and was flourishing by the 1920s. It is said that it was here that Robert Cedric Sherriff, author of Journey's End, the greatest of all 1914 war plays, learned his craft.

Sherriff was a member of the Kingston Rowing Club, then based at Ravens Ait, Surbiton. The club was running out of money and as a fundraising exercise, Sherriff undertook to write plays. These were successful and were staged at The Gables Theatre by the Kingston Adventurers Dramatic Society, according to Margaret Bellars' book, Kingston Then and Now.

The book records that the theatre seated about 250 people and until 1927 was gas-lit. Soon afterwards, it was equipped with electricity and renamed Hillcroft Theatre.

Furthermore, a professional repertory company was in residence at the theatre until the building was pulled down prior to the building of the Glenbuck Road flats shortly before the Second World War.

Wilberforce Bryant was born in Plymouth in 1837.

A Plymouth Express train passes Surbiton near South Terrace and South Bank in about 1906.

Surbiton man was Rupert the bear illustrator

FOR 30 years, the world's most famous teddy bear, Rupert, was illustrated and captioned in Surbiton by a much-loved bachelor, Alfred Bestall.

Rupert first appeared in the Daily Express in November 1920 – the creation of Mary Tourtel, wife of the newspaper's editor. When she retired in 1935 due to failing eyesight Mr Bestall, then 43 years old, was employed by the Express to take over. For the following three decades he illustrated and wrote 270 Rupert stories including 40 for annuals, introducing characters such as Tigerlily and the Old Professor.

As a young man, Mr Bestall had obtained a scholarship to Birmingham Central School of Art. In 1914, he attended the London County Council Central School of Art and the following year volunteered to serve in the army. In 1922, and for several years after, he was a freelance illustrator for Punch and Tatler and drew for more than 50 books. Rupert annuals were the first time Alfred wrote and illustrated but he didn't sign any of his artwork until after Mary Tourtel had died in 1948 out of respect to her.

After he was taken on to draw Rupert, Mr Bestall asked the Express staff for the story for the next edition. He was told there wasn't one, so he tried his hand at writing one. It was Rupert, Algy and the Smugglers. It was meant to be a one-off, but he found himself increasingly providing the stories. He also penned many of the rhyming couplets that neatly sat under the sketches in the annuals.

Mr Bestall's Rupert was one of a re-creation. The little bear began to wear the strident red and yellow colours that millions of children and adults associate him with today. In Mr Bestall's Rupert adventures, there were no fairies and magic wands.

A long-serving member of Surbiton Hill Methodist Church, Mr Bestall first lived with his parents,

Alfred Bestall, of Surbiton, at work on Rupert illustrations in his study in 1963.

Guilford Avenue showing Alfred Bestall's former home at No 58.

No 58 Cranes Park in the year 2004.

Arthur and Rebecca, at No 58 Guilford Avenue soon after being demobbed from the army in 1919. The Bestall family moved to Guilford Avenue in 1920 from Woking. Mr Bestall's father was a Methodist minister, and had spent time in India as a missionary. In 1924, his parents went to Southsea before living in Dorchester from 1930-1933. Later, Mr Bestall lived in Sutherland House, Avenue Elmers, and occassionally took rooms in Bloomsbury. When his parents retired in 1934, they bought Stavordale, 58 Cranes Park, Surbiton. Mr Bestall moved in with his mother, Rebecca, after his father died in 1936. Mr Bestall's mother died at the age of 100 in 1964. While in her late 90s, she was still writing poetry.

In January 1966, Alfred moved to Flat 8, Beaconsfield House, 44 Ewell Road, Surbiton Hill. He remained there for 12 years. He was then lent a flat at 16 Oxford Court while the owner "Terry" was abroad. When Terry returned home and got married, Mr Bestall was able to borrow Mildred Turner's flat at 38a Villiers Avenue, though after 1980, he regarded North Wales as his first home. Since 1956, he had owned a cottage at Beddgelert. On one occasion, Paul and Linda McCartney made a special visit to the cottage and were welcomed inside.

When Philip Turner died suddenly in 1981, Mildred moved from Surbiton to No 45 Church Meadow, Long Ditton, where Mr Bestall sometimes stayed when returning to the area from North Wales.

In 2004, Mildred – who had since become Mrs Baird – was living at Leicester House, Ditton Close, Watts Road, Thames Ditton.

A few years before before he died on January 15th 1986 at the Wern Nursing Home in North Wales, Mr Bestall wintered with friends at No 136, Clayton Road, Hook.

Mr Bestall loved North Wales and its stunning countryside. It was where he had spent his secondary school days and subsequent holidays for 65 years. He spent six or seven fortnights a year there before moving to the cottage permanently in 1980. At the age of 90 he broke his hip playing ping-pong.

During his many years in Surbiton, Mr Bestall forged a strong link with the Surbiton Rotary Club which put up a commemorative plaque in Surbiton Library, Ewell Road, in 1996.

Even though he officially retired from the Rupert work in 1965, Mr Bestall continued to draw the front covers of the Rupert annuals until he was 81 years old.

A night to remember

DURING and after the 1939-1945 war, Rupert illustrator Alfred Bestall was a regular visitor to the home of the Posnett family at No 24 Alexandra Drive, Surbiton.

He frequently arrived with a friend, Brian Smith, on Saturday evenings to play bridge with Sydney Posnett and his wife, Edith. The Posnetts had moved to Alexandra Drive in 1940 after being bombed out of their home at No 39 Collingwood Avenue, Tolworth. Daughter Jean, (also known as Wendy) who was 10 years old at the time, has recalled how a 1,000lb bomb fell in the back garden at about 6pm on 9th September 1940 just as her father had returned home from work and had joined his family in the outside air raid shelter.

The house was damaged but not destroyed and after a year in temporary accommodation in Ripley, Surrey, they moved to Alexandra Drive. Mrs Posnett later became head of nearby Grand Avenue School. She had also taught at Moor Lane School.

Mr Bestall would join in the games of bridge around a coal fire burning in the lounge. There was no central heating those days. Jean would sit with the adults in the same room to keep warm in winter. She was required, however, to keep silent and read her book in the corner and not to interrupt their game.

Jean recalled in later life: "One such evening, shortly before Christmas 1945, my mother saw 'Fred' (as they called him) making a sketch on the back of an envelope but thought no more of it at the time. In due course I received through the post a calendar for the year 1946. It was hand-made and consisted of a sheet of cardboard, about nine inches by seven inches, bearing an original Rupert drawing and a small calendar glued to the bottom."

On the reverse side of the card is written, in ink, in Fred's own handwriting, the words: "To Wendy (Jean). All good wishes for Christmas. In memory of certain evenings you have sat through. (forgive the grammar) A.E.B."

"The Rupert drawing is in pen and ink, coloured with watercolour and is surrounded by a border of holly. It is of four players seated round a card table playing a hand of bridge. Three of the players are my mother, my father and Brian and they are reasonable likenesses in each case," said Jean, an only child.

Edith Posnett and Jean.

Sydney and Edith Posnett, Rupert and Brian Smith playing bridge at No 24 Alexandra Drive in 1945.

"In his own seat, Fred has drawn Rupert, and the players are in the course of making their opening bids, with appropriate speech bubbles.

"The table is viewed from over my mother's shoulder and her cards can clearly be seen to include all four aces, all four kings and at least one queen. My father's speech bubble reads, 'Four no trumps'. Brian's reply is 'double', my mother says, 'Oh dear, I don't know what to do,' to which Rupert replies 'Snap!'"

Fortunately, Jean's father had the foresight to frame the artwork which ensured it survived for many more years.

At the age of 74, and living in Limetree Close, Keyworth, Nottingham, Jean (Atkins) still had that wonderful little drawing and described it as one of her most treasured possessions.

She added: "Incidentally, those long winter evenings were perhaps not quite as boring as I may have implied, as they always ended with my father going out to the nearby fish and chip shop to fetch supper for all of us. Rationing would have made it difficult for us to have provided Saturday suppers for two hungry male guests on a regular basis."

The family moved from Alexandra Drive when Mr Posnett retired in 1962. He sold it to the Methodist Church to provide a residence for ministers from Surbiton Hill Methodist Church.

Trio immortalised in the tales of a famous little bear

The Surbiton guides featured in Rupert books

Guides Janet Francksen, Pauline Coates and Beryl Sweet in a photograph taken by Rupert illustrator Alfred Bestall at Surbiton Hill Methodist Church in 1947.

Janet, Pauline and Beryl in another of Alfred Bestall's photos taken to capture the details of the guide uniforms.

THESE three Surbiton guides were the inspiration behind hundreds of Rupert the Bear stories which have lived on in children's bedrooms for decades.

The girls, who all lived in Berrylands, were members of the 10th Surbiton Guides which met at Surbiton Hill Methodist Church, Ewell Road, where Rupert illustrator, Alfred Bestall, was a member.

One day in 1947, the girls plucked up the courage to ask Mr Bestall — "Uncle Fred" — if they could be in his next Rupert story.

Mr Bestall took the idea very seriously and snapped these black and white photographs of the girls under the beech tree which once graced the outside of the church. He was keen to get the detail of the guides' uniform just right for the illustrations he was planning.

The guides were Beryl Sweet, Pauline Coates and Janet Francksen. Beryl, born in 1934, was the youngest of the three children of print compositor Jack Sweet and his wife, Elsie, of No 17 Pine Gardens, Berrylands.

Pauline, born in 1936, the day before the death of King George V, lived as a child at No 16 Pine Gardens and attended Grand Avenue School in Tolworth and later Tolworth Central Girls' School.

Janet lived on the corner of Manor Drive and Berrylands.

All three were Rupert enthusiasts and were over the moon when Mr Bestall took up their suggestion so readily.

"At the time he was always looking for new ideas for his stories," said Beryl in retirement. "I think we went up to speak to him after a church parade one Sunday."

Beryl's cat, Dinky, even found his way into Rupert tales.

A lifetime later, 'girls' look back

ALMOST sixty years after they first appeared in Rupert stories, the three guides made famous by Alfred Bestall still kept in touch, albeit occasionally.

Janet Francksen lived in Aberdeenshire, Scotland, in 2004. After leaving Surbiton as a young woman, she married a German man named Suss and later moved from the London area to Stoke-on-Trent where the couple ran a hotel.

Tragically, Janet's husband was killed in a road accident in 1972 when he returned home on a visit to Germany. She moved to the Isle of Man, where her parents had relocated to, and worked as a physiotherapist and then to a small village outside Aberdeen where she has a home in a woodcutter's cottage.

By co-incidence Janet, who has three sons, was living in retirement only 20 miles away from the home of Pauline Ellingworth (née Coates), another of the famous guides.

Pauline, who married a Methodist minister, Paul, also has three sons, Martin, Richard and Daniel. In 2004 she said she met up with Janet "quite regularly".

Pauline left Surbiton in 1954 to study at Homerton College, Cambridge but returned to Pine Gardens. Her husband was a missionary in South Africa.

Beryl Sweet married Norman Horrocks in 1955. In 1952 she had moved with her parents to Riverside Close, Kingston. After her wedding, the couple lived in Guilford Avenue and later at 21 Waverley Avenue, Berrylands. In 1987, Beryl and Norman moved to Riverside Close, after the death of Beryl's father.

The couple raised two children.

Above: Rupert illustrator Alfred Bestall at the wedding of former girl-guide Beryl Sweet to Norman Horrocks at Surbiton Hill Methodist Church on 2nd April 1955.

Right: One of the Rupert cartoon strips showing the three guides. Janet Francksen, of Berrylands, is depicted in the blonde-haired girl on the left.

Far right: A Rupert cartoon strip from the Daily Express of 4th September 1951.

Rupert and the Pine Ogre—4

The three Guides like the idea of the competition with Rupert. "There are very few pine trees in this wood," says Beryl, "it would be fairer if we showed you where you can find lots more." So Janet takes him and points across a hill.

"There's a whole pine forest over there," she declares. Thanking her, Rupert hurries away. Almost at once there is a shower of rain. "I must shelter for a minute," he murmurs. "There's someone under that big tree. I do believe it's old Gaffer Jarge. I'll join him."

The famous "Rupert" guides Pauline, Beryl and Janet were reunited in August 1972 when they were guests of Alfred Bestall at a Rupert show staged in Victoria Palace, London. Their children accompanied them to the performance.

Above: Beryl and Janet meet up with Alfred Bestall at the 10th Surbiton Guides' 40th anniversary in December 1970.

Left: The reunited guides signed a programme which also bears Alfred Bestall's signature. Above: Pauline, Beryl and Janet at Surbiton in the 1940s.

The reception at H.C. Jones' offices at No 1 Regent Road in the late 1920s.

H.C. Jones' factory at No 43 Regency Road, near Surbiton Lawn Tennis Club. Here, large quantities of bomb boxes were made for the RAF together with cockpits for fighter planes. The factory, which generated its own gas and electricity, occupied the former tithe barn of Regent Farm.

TRADESMEN'S DELIVERY HATCH

THIS patented device is a nest of cupboards fixed in the larder with plate glass doors internally, and the outside of the hatch having self-locking doors opening on the external flank or rear wall of the house. Each compartment is clearly marked "Butcher," "Milkman," etc. The tradesman takes his order from his cupboard in the morning and on delivering the goods into the hatch closes his door, which automatically locks, leaving the goods actually in the larder and visible to the housekeeper or maid but protected from flies and inaccessible from outside.

This labour-saving invention obviates the nuisance of each tradesman knocking twice at the door (first to take his order and secondly to deliver the goods) and allows the occupant of the house to go out without leaving evidence that the house is temporarily unoccupied, as is the case when loaves, etc., are left on the window sill.

VITÆ GLASS.

This glass, which is the only glass yet discovered that will allow the ultra-violet or health-giving rays of the sun to pass through, can be fitted in bathrooms as an extra if desired, thus enabling the owner of the house to take a sun bath in privacy.

Two of H.C. Jones' inventions offered in his Berrylands houses.

Incredible tale of an inventor who built much of Berrylands and Tolworth

Berrylands and Tolworth were until the 1920s a quiet and rural part of Surrey. Within a decade, they would be completely transformed into a huge expanse of suburbia, providing hundreds of homes for commuters and their families.

The man behind this almost unimaginable alteration of the landscape was builder Harry Charles Jones, who came to Surbiton from Herne Hill, south-east London. He bought up two struggling farms around Berrylands and Tolworth in the 1920s and made a fortune erecting the tree-lined streets that can be seen today.

But Mr Jones was more than a developer. He was an inventor, too. He patented many labour-saving devices and introduced them into the new homes — all of which he had personally designed and built chiefly with materials he had made at the company factory set up in the old tithe barn of the former Regent Farm in Regent Road.

The inventions included a rotating cupboard to make the housewife's selection so simple. Sadly, few of them survive today. He also devised a way of making fireplaces that did not require that infuriating and messy task of emptying the ash and cinders. Mr Jones found a way of allowing the spent coals to be discharged into a pit where they could be collected by the dustman. And he built lockable pigeon holes for visiting tradesmen.

Mr Jones' own personally-designed home at No 27 Berrylands, Surbiton, was like a Tomorrow's World showpiece house, crammed with curious inventions and devices way ahead of their time.

"In 1936, he had a dishwasher, sunken baths and full central heating behind special panels," said his grandson, Rod, who was still running his grandfather's business at 127 Chiltern Drive, Berrylands, in the year 2004.

"He became very wealthy but his main thing in life was seeing a problem and solving it," said Rod.

"During the war, he manufactured a special type of munitions box en masse from the factory at Regent Road, together with lifeboats for the Navy and cockpits for the fighter planes. The bomb boxes were made from timber and steel."

A secondary factory in a 1940 building behind 127 Chiltern Drive was used to a lesser extent in the war effort. Its walls were made of concrete reinforced with iron and railway lines

The man who never slept: Harry Charles Jones.

Shops in Surbiton Hill Park, Berrylands, which H.C. Jones developed in the late 1920s and early 1930s.

and were designed in such a way that if a bomb went off, its roof would lift off, leaving the property generally intact.

When Mr Jones built the Regent Farm estate, he installed a narrow gauge railway used to bring soil down from the higher levels of the land to the lower areas and to convey building materials across the site. It was made in Germany and was run on diesel.

Mr Jones also made his own paint for the new properties. This saved greatly on buying the more expensive proprietory brands, although he did use these makes for the finishing touches. The factory generated its own gas and electricity.

Rod said his grandfather "did not need much sleep and had boundless energy". His company built the whole of the Sunray estate, Surbiton Hill Park, Chiltern Drive, Byways, Berrylands, The Ridings, The Ridge, Hamilton Avenue, Oakleigh Avenue, half of Regent Road, and the road through Tolworth Broadway.

The factory at Regent Road, which occupied the end of the street and ran down Berrylands, was run by the firm from 1920 to 1954. It had a sprung floor covering a labyrinth of pipes.

Mr Jones began his building career in Beckenham and South Norwood turning his attention to Surbiton when the farms went up for sale in the 1920s. He died in 1978.

He left a son, Eric, who took over the business. Eric died in the late 1980s, passing on the firm to his sons Rod and Timothy. In 2004, the firm H.C. Jones was still trading from 127 Chiltern Drive and was concerned purely with property management and property investment.

H.C. Jones' daughter, Edna, was still alive in 2004, living in a retirement home in Dorset and was in her mid nineties.

In retirement, H.C. Jones continued to live at 27 Berrylands. He was in many ways a colourful eccentric. He built a sunken roof with a parapet so he could watch his favourite pastime, tennis, being played at the Surbiton Lawn Tennis Club opposite. He also insisted no-one knew how to wash his clothes properly so he fitted his own washing machine and did his own.

The new cul-de-sac constructed across a field in the bottom left-hand corner in this 1930s photograph was to become Seymour Gardens. On the right are the Surbiton Lawn Tennis Club courts, with the road, Berrylands, running past it up to its junction with The Roystons. On the outer perimeter of the estate is the road Surbiton Hill Park and the railway, beyond which is Lower Marsh Lane.

Park Lodge School, Claremont Road – and rumours of a secret passage

Park Lodge pupils Rosemary Medland; Joan Alexander, head girl; and Beryl Cooper, games captain, in 1947.

PARK LODGE
High School for Girls

(Ages five to eighteen)

ALSO KINDERGARTEN

A SOUND EDUCATION IS IMPARTED
ON MODERN LINES

Girls prepared for the following examinations:

OXFORD LOCAL SCHOOL CERTIFICATE

ROYAL DRAWING SOCIETY

**ASSOCIATED BOARD OF THE ROYAL
ACADEMY OF MUSIC**

THE LONDON ACADEMY OF ELOCUTION

with many successes.

For full details apply to:

The Principal : Miss G. M. FORDHAM

(at Home during term between 3 p.m. and
4 p.m. on Tuesday and Thursday)

35, CLAREMONT ROAD
SURBITON

Telephone : ELMBRIDGE 4249

This advertisement appeared in a Surbiton Borough Council guide book in 1948.

PARK Lodge School was run in the 1940s and 1950s in a large, rambling Victorian villa by three aging spinster sisters, Grace, Louie and Connie Fordham.

Former pupils recall Grace often wearing a plum-coloured skirt and jumper. She would frequently put her hands in her jumper pockets and nervously keep pulling it down while lolling her tongue around her mouth.

Connie was an ex-military nurse and came into the business as a teacher. Louie taught needlework.

The ex-pupils also spoke of a "wisened" old lady, Miss Garlick, who held French, biology and history lessons.

Joan Middlemore, who married and became Joan Hynes, was a pupil between 1943 and 1949. At the time she was living in Ember Lane, Esher, having moved south from Newcastle-Upon-Tyne. She claims her father sent her to Park Lodge because the school had a large cellar where the girls could shelter during air raids in the Second World War. Joan would realise how real the air raid warnings could be, for Ember Court, near her home, was bombed one day.

Joan recalls that in a corner of the cellar was an old bath which covered a deep hole.

"It was rumoured that there were secret passages that led to the river," she said in retirement, looking back to her Surbiton schooldays.

Joan recalled the headmistress being "very elderly". In fact, she said, many of the staff were getting on in years, probably because of the shortage of younger teachers during the war years.

In the garden of the school was a large cedar tree, which provided shade on hot summer days. Sometimes lessons were held outside in hot weather.

"The playground was marked out for netball and tennis. There was also a fig tree in the garden.

In the winter, a shortage of coal in the 1940s meant lessons were often held in cold classrooms.

"There were solid-fuel boilers and when there was no fuel, we sat there shivering in our coats," said Joan, who lived in early retirement at Echo Barn Lane, Farnham.

"Once, there was only one fire lit in the building. It was in the dining room, so lessons were held there in the morning, the tables were cleared for lunch and then again for afternoon lessons.

"What namby pambies we are today in comparison," commented Joan.

Occasionally, Joan has stumbled across other former pupils in her travels.

Once, she was in Westminster, London, and had been sightseeing when she stopped for lunch. She got talking to a woman sitting nearby. It turned out to be former Park Lodge pupil Joan Cattermole. After leaving the school, Miss Cattermole married and moved to the United States for a time.

Beryl Cooper, who married a Geoffrey Havers, was a classmate of Joan Middlemore. She, too, had some amusing anecdotes to share.

She recalled that the girls in the class would play up to Miss Garlick by hiding in cupboards. "The teacher would ask: 'Where's so and so today?' and the girls would be in stitches because they knew the others were hiding in the cupboards. When she had her back to the class, we'd all edge up our desks a few inches closer to the front and she would turn round and say: 'You're all a bit close aren't you?' and there'd be a big racket as everyone dragged their desks backwards."

Pupils under the cedar tree in the garden of Park Lodge School, Claremont Road, in the late 1940s. In the top row, left to right, are Mary Trehearn, Daphne Field and Pat Burrows. In the middle row are Anne Wrathall, Rosemary Medland, Joan Alexander and Erica Thon. Kneeling at the front are Pauline Hurst and Joan Middlemore.

Schoolfriends reunited

THANKS to a hugely successful site on the worldwide web, a lot of old schoolfriends have got back in touch again. Friends Reunited enables people to make contact with former classmates who have registered with the website.

It is possible to select a school and your final year and see who else has registered. By paying a small annual subscription, messages can be sent to long-lost pals.

In early 2004, seven 'old' girls of Park Lodge School, Claremont Road, Surbiton, had signed up to Friends Reunited.

Happily, they were then able to exchange news about each other.

The subscribers included Christine Moore, Geraldine "Gerry" Evans, Mary Ferris, Wendy Chalk, Angela Coffee and Susan Warner. They left the school in the mid to late 1950s.

Christine Moore in the year 2003 told friends she had raised three children in the intervening 50 years. Two of her children were married and her daughter had just had her first baby. She spent most of the year in Majorca with her second husband but had a flat in Guildford.

In 2002, Mary Ferris informed her old classmates that she was living in St Albans and had three grown-up sons "one of whom refuses to leave home". She had worked for the previous 10 years in the IT industry. She still revisited Surrey regularly to catch up with friends and had taken up golf as she was finding tennis hard work.

Angela Coffee, another former Park Lodge pupil was living at Church Crookham in Hampshire in 2003. She said that after leaving school, she went to work in London for Thorns and then BOAC for eight years. She married and had three children and was working at a local primary school in Fleet.

She said she was in contact with Jane Nightingale, Mary Farrer and Pam Ross-Symons.

Susan Walker wrote in 2003 that she had worked in the travel industry for five years but had previously had another job for 22 years. Her parents had run a wallpaper shop in Ham Parade.

Susan had a son, William, aged 24, who worked with schoolchildren. Her sister, Elizabeth, also went to Park Lodge and remembered Angela Coffee and some of the others.

Trolley bus wires hang across the road on the approach to Surbiton Station in the late 1950s. In about 1960, the Southampton Hotel, pictured on the left, was demolished and a new public house was built on the site with the towering Winthrop House offices above. Lightfoot's, the jeweller's, trades in the centre of the single-storey parade in front of the clock-tower.

Actor Francis Matthews

Comedian Ronnie Barker was just one of the famous guests at Francis Matthews' 70th birthday party in 1997. Ernie Wise also attended. Ronnie (left) is pictured with Francis.

FRANCIS Matthews, an actor known throughout the world, used to live at No 33 Hook Road in the early 1950s. Perhaps best known for his appearances as Paul Temple in the 1969 TV detective series of the same name, Francis lived with his parents, Harry and Kitty, at the Edwardian house between Thornhill Road and Maypole Motors. Mr and Mrs Matthews were from Yorkshire where Francis, the second youngest of four children, was born in 1927. The other siblings were Paul, Maura and Anthony.

Harry, who was awarded an OBE, worked for the General and Municipal Workers' Union in London and became a national officer. Co-incidentally, the General Secretary of the GMWU, Lord Thomas Williamson CBE lived in No 10 Kingsdowne Road, just half a mile from the Matthews family.

Francis starred in scores of films including Bhowani Junction (1956). His youngest brother, Paul (Shelley) born in 1942, also became an actor.

Francis lived permanently with his family in Hook Road for only a year or so. His career was taking off with a vengeance. He moved to a flat in Earls Court and when he married Angela Browne in 1963, London became his main home. Their son, Damien Matthews, followed in his father's career.

The Matthews family lived in Hook Road from 1950 to the 1970s when they moved to a flat at 92 Ditton Road. Harry died in 1982; Kitty in 1984.

The Hook Road house was said to be "solid with dark panelling."

Peggy Schutters and Petula Clark meet Down Under in 2004.

Oz reunion for Petula Clark

THEY first met at an end-of-war street party in Vallis Way, Hook, in 1945. Almost 60 years later, world-famous singer Petula Clark who performed at that party as a girl, met up with Peggy Windsor — now Schutters — who was one of the children in attendance.

Their remarkable encounter was at the Twin Towns Services Club at Tweed Heads, New South Wales, Australia, on 28th February 2004.

Petula, who lived with her father and manager, Leslie Clark, at "Don Tor", Salmons Road, Chessington, in the 1940s and attended Moor Lane School, was touring Australia. Peggy had moved Down Under in 1963 with her husband Wilhelm, a Dutchman who fled to England during his own country's occupation by the Germans.

The concert was a sell-out and the audience gave Petula a rousing welcoming reception. After the show, she met and signed more than 200 fans' autographs in the star lounge.

All those years ago, Petula would often be seen waiting for friends outside Surbiton Station in her distinctive pink sports car with its personalised registration number. On one occasion she dyed her hair pink to match it.

As a girl, Petula had a number of friends in the Hook and Chessington area. She sang at many local events in the district.

In the 1940s, Peggy lived at No 42 Somerset Avenue, Hook. Her brother, Alan, joined the Post Office and worked at the Elm Road branch after it was opened in 1955. In retirement, Alan lived in Northamptonshire.

Eric Clapton

ONE of the world's best-known rock guitarists, Eric Clapton, attended Hollyfield School as an art student.

In the lunch hour, if the weather was fine, he would sometimes strum a guitar surrounded by school friends in the Alexandra Recreation Ground. The students would munch on sandwiches as Clapton entertained them as much as once a week in the summer.

Clapton.

The star lived with his grandmother at Ripley Green, where he was born in 1945.

Some of the art lessons were held in an off-site classroom in Ewell Road, Surbiton Hill. Clapton also studied stained-glass design at Kingston Art School.

Ingrid Holford

AUTHOR and meteorologist Ingrid Holford and her family lived in the 1960s and 1970s at No 32 Hook Road at a house called Westernhay.

Among her books were British Weather Disasters and The Guinness Book of Weather. Her

Ingrid Holford.

in-laws lived at Southernhay, Hook Road, in the 1930s. It was there that author Enid Blyton lived 1920-1924.

Surbiton District Girl Guides' summer camp at West Wittering, Sussex, in 1929.

Surbiton Guides at camp

O NE of Surbiton and Tolworth's thriving guide groups was the 5th Surbiton (St Matthew's), which was formed in about 1917.

The girls met in St Matthew's Hall in Douglas Road, Tolworth. For many years the guides' captain was Miss K Rands, of 51 Douglas Road. She was in the early days of the company a radiographer at London's St Thomas's Hospital but transferred to Surbiton Hospital when it opened in Ewell Road in July 1936. The guides formed a guard of honour for the Duke of Gloucester at the opening ceremony.

Marion Gardner was one of those girls. At the age of 86 in 2004, she recalled: "It was a terrible day for weather and we

were soaked through. At the end we were given a glass of lemonade."

Marion, who became Mrs Knocks and in retirement lived at Caversham, said: "At camps we learned how to cook on open fires. We had enormous great dixies full of stew. We would fan the flames with tin plates. For washing, we put up canvas stands by twisting string around sticks. We'd put our flannels on the canvas."

She added that the camps at Wittering were on a farm. The farmer was also a guide leader who used to walk around with a goat on a lead.

Connie Pratt, of Raeburn Avenue, helped lead the guides.

Serving up a steamed pudding cooked on an open fire by Surbiton Guides in the inter-war era.

Surbiton guides at their summer camp in Peper Harrow, near Godalming, in 1928 are pictured above. The smaller pictures show scenes from the girls' similar camps in the 1920s and 1930s.

Surbiton Guides on one of their inter-war seaside summer camps.

Recalling the 'old' girls after guide log books re-emerge in the 21st century

LOG books of the 5th Surbiton Guides dating back some 75 years recently came back into the hands of Surbiton historians after they were found on sale on the internet. The seller was pleased they had found a good home, however, following a house clearance sale in the Surbiton area.

The log books list all the members of the guide company, give their addresses and list the badges they achieved.

The girls met at St Matthew's Hall in Douglas Road, Tolworth, and the books refer to the period 1927 to 1935.

Octogenarians and nonegenarians in and around Tolworth were thrilled to be shown the books. The names of the girls brought back a flood of happy memories.

Here is a list of some of the girls: Peggy Brown, 15a Tankerton Road; Laura Ebdon, 19 Ravenscar Road, born 11th September 1911; Connie Blench, 123 Douglas Road, born 3rd December 1913; Eileen Johnson, 17 Tankerton Road, born 21st April 1913; Kathleen Johnson, 17 Tankerton Road, born 6th April 1914; Connie Yarlett, 174 Thornhill Road, born 5th January 1913; Ellen Darby, 60 Bond Road, born 5th March 1914; Joan Buller, 86 Beaconsfield Road, born 13th October 1914; Madeline Drake, 7 Birchington Road, born 13th April 1915; Vera Kirby, 69 Douglas Road, born 23rd August 1915; Gwen Robbins, 114 Douglas Road, born 29th March 1915; Florrie Newman, 94 Tolworth Park Road, born 30th September 1914; Mabel Harris, 8 Douglas Road, born 30th September 1912; Nona Voller, 41 Bond Road, born 25th February 1915; Winnie Austin, 63 Douglas Road, born 1st October 1914; Gladys Page, 102 Ellerton Road, born 31st July 1915; Elsie Waters, 79 Bond Road, born July 31st 1914; Florence Rising, 261 Ewell Road, born 18th September 1916; Renee Harris, 8 Douglas Road, born 13th December 1916; Sylvia Thorogood, 11 Kingsmead Avenue, born 20th April 1917; Doris Turner, 302 Ewell Road, born 6th January 1917; Vera Maslin, 32 Douglas Road, born 17th April 1913; Gladys Newman, 100 Beaconsfield Road, born 25th August 1916; Violet Ambrose, 106 Thornhill Road, born 24th July 1914; Joan Wyatt, 25 Worthington Road, born 24th December 1915; Margaret Wyatt, 85 Fullers Avenue; born 30th December 1916; D. King, 9 Douglas Road; Irene Marlton, 28 Berrylands Road, born 20th April 1917; Ivy Davis, 28 Bond Road, born 23rd August 1915; Marie Catford, 167 Thornhill Road, born 7th January 1916; Ivy Crocker, 17 Ravenscar Road, born 27th September 1916; Dorothy Paveley, 11 King Charles Road, born 27th April 1915; Mary Jones, 21 Dennan Road, 12th April 1916; Joan Martin, 42 Fullers Avenue, born 23rd September 1916; Doris Page, 102 Ellerton Road, born 11th September 1916; Winifred Ambrose, 6 Hill Crescent, born 7th June 1916; Dorothy Nicholas, 169 Thornhill Road, born 11th June 1915; Edith Ransom, 76 Fullers Avenue, born 12th January 1917. Phyllis Hall, 199 Red Lion Road, born 2nd September 1917; Maisie Etches, Tower House Garage, Browns Road, born 5th May 1915; K. O'dell, 91 Fullers Avenue, born 16th December 1917; G. Sharp, 163

Thornhill Road, born 2nd April 1916; Marion Morgan, 17 Hamilton Avenue, born 22nd September 1916; Muriel Fletcher, 98 Douglas Road, born 2nd December 1916; M. Ceely, 36 St Mark's Hill, born 25th October 1915; Ruth Hall, 21 Tolworth Park Road, born 10th August 1918. E. Garlett, 174 Thornhill Road, born 16th April 1916; Frances Brown, 136 Tolworth Road, born 26th July 1917; Maisie Farmer, 27 Cranbourne Avenue, born 31st May 1918; Doris Phenna, 186 Ellerton Road, born 23rd August 1917; Joan Lamb, 374 Ewell Road, born 25th November 1917; K(?), Johnson, 17 Tankerton Road, born 26th December 1917; Helen Rising 261 Ewell Road, born 5th February 1918; Audrey Aggett, 59 Beaconsfield Road, born 8th August 1918; Doris Page, 102 Ellerton Road, born 11th September 1916; Joan Thorn, 2 Fullers Avenue, born 15th March 1917; Doris Middleditch, 24 Raeburn Avenue, born 24th April 1917; Betty Greenwood, 1 Raeburn Avenue, born 21st February 1918; Dora Scears, 2 Largewood Avenue, born 9th December 1916; Molly Dibble, 122 Ellerton Road, born 25th September 1917; Emily Pearson, 51 Princes Avenue, born 5th October 1916; Gladys Wollaston, Rossyln, Ewell Road, born 28th March 1915; Molly Burton, 39 Fullers Avenue, born 27th December 1918; Marion Gardner, 47 Kingsmead Avenue, born 31st January 1918; Lucy Pilgrim, 9 Pyne Road, born 30th May 1917; Peggy Day, 160 Red Lion Road, born 1st February 1918; Freda Read, 117 Largewood Avenue, born 15th January 1916; Vera Garrett, 12 Tankerton Road, born 28th September 1916; Lydia Ambrose, Hill Crescent; Kathleen Cadle, 156 Thornhill Road, born 2nd September 1918; Joan Martin, 115 Douglas Road, born 10th March 1917; I. Hayes, 160 Douglas Road, born 8th November 1919; Doris Crocker, 17 Ravenscar Road, born 30th January 1920; Joyce Barlow, Corner House, King Charles Road, born 22nd November 1919; Dorothy Chipsham, 41 Ravenswood Avenue, born April 16th 1918; Margaret Viveash, 140 Hook Road, born 5th June 1917; Mary Drakeford, 17 Brook Road, Hook, born 27th July 1918; Letetia Quartermain, 88 Tolworth Road, born 5th November 1917; Pamela Gray, Inglenook, Cotterill Road, born 23rd May 1919; Eva Bull, 68 Ellerton Road, born 27th May 1919; Joyce Waddington, 186 Douglas Road, born 24th July 1919; Flossie Spencer, Avalaon, Kingsdowne Road, born 11th July 1920; Doreen Vine, 72 Ellerton Road, born 19th May 1920; Joyce Shearman, 12 Derby Road, born 2nd December 1921; Christine Wyeth, Tolworth Recreation Ground, born 17th September 1921; Dorothy Yarlett, 54 Priory Road, Hook, born 27th April 1921; Doris Robinson, 125 Cranbourne Avenue, 12th February 1920; Joan Smith, 19 Brook Road, Hook, born 5th May 1920; Vera Ryder, 54 Ravenswood Avenue, born 13th November 1921; Joan Fagan, 19 Broomfield Road, 4th April 1920; Joyce Newman, 106 Thornhill Road, born 5th September 1920; Joyce Little, 367 Ewell Road, born 26th May 1918; Doris Martin, 42 Fullers Avenue, born 25th August 1920; E. Locke, 71 Worthington Road, born 1st May 1922; Madge Buller, 86 Beaconsfield Road, born 20th December 1920; Lilian Holland, 164 Thornhill Road, born 19th June 1921; Joan Locke, 71 Worthington Road, born 2nd February 1920; Doris Newstead, 93 Raeburn Avenue, born 16th June 1918; Vera Austin, 63 Douglas Road, born 6th March 1920; Gladys Carr, 67

The 5th Surbiton (St Matthew's) Guides joined up with the 10th Surbiton for their 1937 camp in Earnley, near Bracklesham Bay, Sussex. The girls from the 5th wore dark green ties while the girls from the10th sported light-coloured ones. Pip the dog, seen in the picture, accompanied the girls on many of their camps in the 1930s. Pictured in the top row, left to right, are Miss M. Rands, Miss Wallis, Miss Toreville, Miss C. Pratt, Miss V. Gridley, J. Buller and M. Rutterford. In the centre row are D. Martin, B. Wood, E. Tournay, M. Edwards, M. Sims, M. Gardner and E. Bull. In the front row are J. Lanham, J. Guy, M. Davies, P. Saul, M. Tarring, C. New, M. Bolde and, B Cheney.

Ravenswood Avenue, born 29th July 1920; Nancy Davies, 61 Largewood Avenue, born 24th July 1919; Lily Bridge, 160 Thornhill Road, born 5th April 1923; Betty Cheney, 27 Vincent Avenue, born 18th February 1924; Barbara Hayes, 160 Douglas Road, born 20th May 1921; Kathleen Durnsford, 123 Tolworth Road, born 17th December 1921; Diane Craddock, 17 Largewood Avenue, born 16th November 1920; Betty Cadell, 19 Ravenswood Avenue, born 7th April 1922; Audrey Parratt, 77 Ronelean Road, born 22nd April 1920; Joan Ryder, 54 Ravenswood Avenue, born 22nd December 1921; Joan Milton, 129 Douglas Road, born 1st August 1924; Jean Groves, 62 Ladywood

Avenue, born 1st July 1923; Muriel Bolden, 70 Cotterill Road, born 10th May 1923; Margaret Shipp, 201 Douglas Road, born 10th June 1924; Joan Whitening, 1 Fullers Avenue, born 28th December 1919; Violet Greene, 142 Hook Rise, born 3rd December 1919; Joan Harrison, 62 Bond Road, born 25th August 1920; Peggy Milton, Tolworth Park Road, born 26th October 1922; Irene Rice, 38 Ronelean Road, born 8th August 1924; Marie Tarring, 9 Ravenswood Avenue, born 9th July 1924; Leila Tinsley, 68 Ladywood Road, born 1st August 1924; Peggy Godfrey, 55 Ravenswood Avenue, born 11th September 1924; Phyllis Damian, 96 Largewood Avenue, born 9th March 1925; Joan Guy, 100 Largewood Avenue, born 3rd April 1925; Joyce Hayes, 160 Douglas Road, born December 1 1924; Margaret Monk, 61 Hamilton Avenue, 28th May 1924; Marjorie Davies, 158 Red Lion Road, born 18th February 1925; Audrey Fairhead, Ellerton Road, born 30th June 1925; Lily Mager, 29 Ravenswood Avenue, born 5th September 1923; Joyce Maddison, 35 Vincent Avenue, born 6th November 1925; Jean Bell, 52 Kingsmead Avenue, born 4th June 1926; Joan Lanham, 27 Ravenswood Avenue, born 25th September 1925; and Phyllis Scholfield, 13 Ravenswood Avenue, born 6th May 1925.

Marion Gardner, of Kingsmead Avenue, Tolworth, was one of the 5th Surbiton (St Matthew's) guides in the 1930s.
In the year 2004, Mrs Marion Knocks, of Caversham, Berks, (the same 'girl') reminisced about those happy days of her youth. The guide captain in her group was Miss K. Rands.

Top cyclist who was son of a window cleaner

In the early 1950s, Brian Loder of 17 Arlington Road, Surbiton, was an award-winning racing cyclist and was the first member of the Molesey-based Clarence Wheelers to achieve 25 miles in less than an hour. Brian's father, Harold, was Surbiton's omnipresent window cleaner. Brian, a signwriter, married cleric's daughter Anne Lacey and moved to Fordgate in Somerset where he died in recent years. He had a son, Robert.

Surbiton postmen

Several Surbiton postmen from the early 1950s are in this team photograph of the Kingston Postal Football Club. They include Les Clapson (top row, far left) Bobby Amlett (top row, fourth from the left) Keith Coughtree (top row, far right) Jimmy Punter (bottom row, second from the right) and Denny Gill (bottom row, far left).

Slain on Surbiton Hill

MATCH company chairman Wilberforce Bryant, had been living at The Gables, South Bank, Surbiton, for 11 years when his fortunes were threatened by a strike at his factory in east London.

In 1888, Wilberforce was confronted with the fact that many of the girls working for Bryant and May were suffering from an illness caused by too much contact with phosphorus. The women had gone on strike after conditions at the factory were criticised by reformers of the time.

Bryant left Surbiton and the house was bought by Arthur Cooper, a private doctor to the Prince of Wales.

The magnate's wealth was not too dented by events, however. Bryant bought Stoke Park, an impressive country estate near Stoke Poges in Buckinghamshire. The manor house at Stoke Park was built by the Second Earl of Huntingdon in 1555. One third of the manor can still be seen today and the park is the home of a beautiful golf course.

By coincidence, Stoke Park has a strong royal link with Surbiton. The Buckinghamshire property was owned by Sir John Villiers between 1644 and 1656. John's brother, George, was King Charles I's closest friend. George's sons, George Villiers (1628-1687) the second Duke of Buckingham, and Francis Villiers (born in about 1628) were raised by the king after their father was assassinated at Portsmouth in 1628. In 1648, Francis Villiers was killed in a Civil War battle at Surbiton. Villiers Road and Villiers Avenue recall the slain young man.

Frances Coke, who lived at Stoke Park in the early 1600s, was once locked up in the mansion by her father, a former owner of Stoke Park, until she agreed to marry Sir John Villiers.

During the Civil War, when parliamentarians were fighting the Royalists, the king was briefly held prisoner at Stoke Park on a journey from York to London in January 1647. On 14th August, the king was removed from Stoke Park to Hampton Court and was received as a prisoner in the custody of his own subjects.

The king escaped from Hampton Court in 1648 and one version of events is that he managed to cross the River Thames and reach the Surbiton bank where horses awaited him to facilitate his escape.

During this turbulent time, an army of Cromwell's men were travelling north after skirmishes in the Reigate, Dorking and

The Duke of Buckingham public house, Villiers Road, in 2004. The hostelry's name, as that of the road, recalls a battle in the Civil War when Lord Francis Villiers, brother of the Duke of Buckingham, was killed at Surbiton Common in July 1648. Inset: The Duke of Buckingham as a child in the 1630s.

Lord Francis Villiers.

Nonsuch area and had reached Surbiton Common, which in those days was a large area of heath and gorse between the south of Kingston and Hook.

Here, on 6th July 1648, there was a battle. Three divisions of Royalists had taken up position on top of Surbiton Hill and were fired upon by Parliamentary soldiers hiding in bushes. The Earl of Holland led a futile Royalist charge, using 50 horses. But the Parliamentary forces advanced from behind with a strength that had not been anticipated. The Royalists were utterly outnumbered in soldiers, horses and ammunition and defeat was quick.

It was reported that 20 Royalist officers and soldiers were killed, the Earl of Holland was injured, 200 were hurt, 100 were taken prisoner and 200 horses were captured and removed. The earl was fiercely criticised for his failed tactics.

Among the dead was 19-year-old Lord Francis Villiers, the king's "adopted" son. He was said to have been a remarkably good-looking youth.

It was chronicled that he was killed in a lane between Kingston and Surbiton Common while trying to resist arrest. As his horse was slaughtered under him, Villiers turned his back to an elm tree and "fought most valiantly with half a dozen". The enemy pounced from behind a hedge, knocked off his helmet and killed him. The Duke of Buckingham later escaped to Holland after being "surprised" at St Neots four days later.

The Surbiton battle is reported to have occurred between six and seven o'clock in the evening. Francis's body, riddled with wounds, was carried by boat up the Thames from Kingston to the Strand in London and having there been embalmed, was deposited in his father's vault in the chapel of Henry VI at Westminster.

After the crushing of the new Royalist resistance, King Charles I was taken to London to be tried and was beheaded at the Palace of Westminster the following year.

Historians have often tried to pinpoint the location of the spot where Lord Francis Villiers lost his life. Some have suggested it was along what is now Villiers Path.

The Duke of Buckingham pub, Villiers Road and Avenue, and King Charles' Road, Surbiton, all recall the battle.

A wartime childhood

Alan Davis was born on 3rd May 1937 at Tolworth Nursing Home, Tolworth Rise. His entry into the world came just nine days before the coronation of King George VI on 12th May.

Alan was the second child of Walter and Alice Davis, who lived in a semi-detached bungalow at No 11 Northcote Avenue, off Raeburn Avenue. The family also had a collie dog called Laddie.

In retirement, Mr Davis looked back fondly on his childhood days in Surbiton, but with war being declared when he was only two and a half years old, there were many worrying times for his family and their neighbours.

Mr Davis recalls many of the neighbours when he was a boy in Northcote Avenue. He remembered a Mr and Mrs Bell living at No 9. The Bells had a son, Brian, who was about two years older than himself.

At No 13 lived the Andrews family. One of the sons was called Vernon, recalled Mr Davis. In No 15 resided Tom Berryman and his wife.

Alan also remembered a Mr Harry Scott at No 23, whom he believed was a company director. He lived at the house with his wife and was the only man in the road who owned a car.

Other neighbours recalled by Mr Davis included the Fields, (No 25), the Vinsons (No 27), the Chessmans (No 31), the Browns (No 35), the Neales (No 39), the Mitchells and the Hogbins. On the other side the neighbours included the Willetts (No 36), Tom Berryman's mother (No 32), and the Evans family.

Mrs Court occupied No 26 along with Billy and Vera Court. Billy was "a big boy we all looked up to" said Mr Davis. The Grimblys were at No 28.

Alan's sister Sheila was next on the scene. She was born on 7th January 1939 also at the Tolworth Nursing Home, Nos 85 and 87 Tolworth Rise.

On Sunday 3rd September 1939, war was declared against Nazi Germany. It must have been a fretful time for a mother with two very young children and a dog who was energetic enough to leap over a tall side gate.

"I can't remember what happened to Laddie. I suspect that he was either given away or put to sleep," said Alan.

During the war, Alan's father, who worked for the building firm Thorogood, served in the auxiliary fire service as he was

The Davis children of Northcote Avenue. From left to right, Sheila, Jennifer, Tony and Alan.

in what was called a reserved occupation. Thorogood & Sons built hundreds, if not thousands, of houses in the area.

Walter Davis cycled three miles to work each day to his company's site where he carried out a full day's work before going to the city of London where he would spend the night on duty with the fire brigade, putting out blazes and rescuing people trapped in buildings which had collapsed during the bombing campaigns. This exhausting routine continued throughout the war years.

Walter's parents, Arthur and Edith, lived close to the family, at No 67 Endway. Arthur was a retired station officer with the fire brigade and during the Second World War served as an Air

Raid Precautions (ARP) warden. The warden's job was to check that all blackouts were in place and report fires and bomb damage.

The blackouts were formed from thin sheets of plywood positioned against the insides of windows to prevent house lights showing up to enemy aircraft, so giving away positions of towns during night-time air raids. The wardens were responsible for their own neighbourhoods and also made sure people were in their shelters when air raid warnings were sounded.

Alan's recollections of the war years and his time at school are continued on the next few pages.

Raising a family during the war

Bombs, blasts and babies

FAMILY life in Northcote Avenue went on despite terrifying bomb raids in the Berrylands and Tolworth area which resulted in several houses being demolished and almost 60 people being killed in the district.

The Davis family at No 11 increased in size as one more child arrived in February 1941. On the 12th, Anthony came into their world and provided a brother for Alan and a sister for Sheila.

As bombs hurtled out of the sky from German planes and exploded in the neighbourhood, killing more than 57 people in the Surbiton borough, Kathleen Davis struggled to feed three hungry young mouths all under the age of five.

The nearest bomb to fall in the vicinity of the family's home at Northcote Avenue was the one which descended on Surbiton Lagoon. The pool was used as a reservoir for fire-fighting at the time.

A shelter had been built in the Davis family's garden. It consisted of a four-feet deep pit with cemented walls and a corrugated iron roof which was covered in clay. It had a tall brick wall at the side, facing the opening, to shield occupants from bomb blast.

In the shelter the family felt fairly secure but if it have taken a direct hit, death and injury would have been likely.

Alan recalled: "My one lingering memory of this time is the smell of Swan Vestas matches which my mum must have used to light the candles. I can also remember her telling me to come into the shelter when I was more interested in watching the planes overhead, as she thought the pilots could have seen a little boy peeping. This type of shelter was called an Anderson, as opposed to a Morrison which was indoors and had a heavy angle frame and thick steel plate roof. The sides were made of steel rectangular mesh.

"Our one was covered with a large velvet-type table cloth with tassels hanging around the edges. I think it was a sort of brown colour. The purpose of this shelter was to protect the occupants from falling timber and masonry."

Sometimes Kathleen would take the children to Sydenham, south-east London, by bus to visit their nan. Alan recalls a three-hour journey starting with a trip to Mitcham on the 152 from the Kingston bypass.

RALEIGH DRIVE, TOLWORTH.

Raleigh Drive, Tolworth, in the 1930s when only one or two people in the road owned a car.

"Nan taught us a silly rhyme which went: 'Annie Marire put her bot in the fire; it was too hot, she burnt her bot." My mum thought it was too rude to pass on to children."

It was in London that Alan was fascinated to see barrage balloons for the first time. Their aim was to interfere with German planes and prevent them bombing or machine gunning sensitive targets.

Alan's grandfather, Albert Eatwell, would sit listening to the news on a wireless during the children's visits and get grumpy if he couldn't hear the broadcast. It was a type of "cat's whisker" radio — one of the first radios made.

In the summer of 1942, Alan started school. This was at Grand Avenue Primary School, Tolworth.

"I remember I was taken there by a big girl called Monica Burstow who lived over the road from us. As the war was still on, Mum said that if the sirens started before we crossed Raeburn Avenue, we were to come home. If we had crossed the road we were to run to school.

"Whilst at school, we had drills to evacuate the school as quickly as possible, the little ones leaving first.

"We were all led into air raid shelters along one edge of the playing field, class by class.

"When we were all in the shelters, Miss Toms, the headmistress, used to patrol up and down outside with a long white stick, presumably to beat the hell out of any bombs which dared to land near her charges.

"Miss Toms, as I recall, was a small lady, very slender with her hair pulled back and shaped into a bun.

"Among the teachers I clearly remember was Miss Pratt, Mrs Jenkins, Miss Stephens and Mrs Wasserburg. Miss Pratt took the younger ones under her wing. Mrs Jenkins, of class six, taught in upstairs classrooms and lived in a corner bungalow near the school. Miss Stephens was a Canadian supply teacher who took class seven and Mrs Wasserburg had class eight."

Street parties to celebrate end of the war

Families in Ladywood Avenue, Tolworth, celebrating VE day at the end of war with a street party in 1945.

Scarlet fever and isolation

Alan Davis was enjoying school life at Grand Avenue, Tolworth, during the Second World War. Some of the lessons taken by Mrs Wasserburg were held in a hut beside Emmanuel Church. His favourite teacher was a Mrs King who lived at No 59 Raeburn Avenue. She taught the boys football and cricket for which they had to supply the equipment. The reason a woman teacher was instructing the youngsters in sport was the fact that most able-bodied male teachers were still in the services, fighting for their country in the war.

It was during 1944 that Alan caught scarlet fever.

"I remember being rushed off to Tolworth Isolation Hospital by ambulance, covered in a fluffy red blanket. Scarlet fever at that time was considered extremely contagious."

Two of Alan's friends, Brian Hughes and Sheila Neale, also caught it. As it was still wartime, when the sirens sounded the children had to get under the ward beds and lie on a mattress on the floor until the all-clear was given.

"When I was visited by my mum and dad or anyone else I couldn't touch them and they had to talk to me through an open fanlight window.

"None of my brothers or sisters caught this disease. I think I stayed in hospital for about six to eight weeks then I had to stay with my nan for a further few weeks. I remember the hospital had a classroom, so none of us escaped lessons. I also recall my parents bringing in my favourite teddy bear. When I left hospital, he had to be incinerated. I was only seven at the time.

"Brian Hughes remained a friend until I left school and went to work. Sheila Neale was always around, a friend and neighbour for many years until I joined the army and lost touch. I remember it was Sheila who showed me that girls were different to boys and what that difference was, although I didn't appreciate it at the time, being only about nine years old.

"After I left hospital in 1944, the three of us children were evacuated to Aspley Guise in Bedfordshire. Here we lived in a wooden building behind a Baptist Church attended by my great uncle. Pastor Davis was the minister and we called him Uncle Chum and his wife, Auntie Em. Whilst we were there, all three of us caught a bad attack of fleas. I can still visualise Mum washing our hair with some obnoxious shampoo and cracking the fleas between her thumbnails saying: 'That's

Alan Davis's grandparents Arthur and Edith Davis who lived for many years at No 67 Endway, Surbiton. Alan adored them.

another one'. We caught the fleas from the mice we heard running about at night over the bedclothes of the double bed we all slept in.

"In 1944, Hitler launched his doodlebugs or V1s. We would pray that the engines would not cut out while they were above us and come down over us. By October of that year, the threat seemed to have passed after their launch sites on the continent were destroyed by our armies.

"On 2nd November, my second sister, Jennifer was born at 11 Northcote Avenue. Our family now seemed complete with two boys and two girls. When each of them was born, I was sent up the road to stay with my beloved nan and grandad, Arthur and Edith Davis at 67 Endway, Surbiton.

"On June 6 1944, the Allies landed in Europe and within a year had cleared the continent of Nazi troops or at least had captured them. The war in Europe officially ended on May 8 1945. I remember that my mum received a telegram from her mother stating that my mum's brother, Bert, was safe and well. Bert had been a prisoner of war having been captured by the Japanese when Singapore fell to them. When we saw him on his return we were amazed at how thin he was. His legs looked like bones.

"A few weeks after the war ended, street parties and all manner of celebrations were held.

"At the street party in Northcote Avenue, food not seen for years was displayed on tables in front of excitable children. In the evening, bonfires were lit and music was played. The adults all danced to the hit tunes of the day. I remember dancing with Mrs Berryman to Run Rabbit Run, Run Run, Don't Give the farmer his gun, gun, gun. He'll get by without his rabbit pie So Run Rabbit Run Rabbit, Run Run Run."

There was also a celebratory party in the grounds of the Grand Avenue School. Parents dressed up as the United Nations in their national dress. The youngsters carried a board with the words "united nations" on it and in a picture taken at the time, it shows Alan holding the sign the wrong way around." The United Nations had just formed in October 1945.

In 1946, the family decided to move home, but not far. They relocated to No 32 and old Mrs Berryman moved across the road to the Davis family's bungalow. Alan recalls helping his dad dig up an apple tree and move it along the road into No 32. This tree grew and provided fine cooking apples in later years. Alan's father planted further trees which provided pears and plums. The plum tree was next to the part of the garden where chickens were kept for their eggs. Soon, Alan's dad built a conservatory on the back of the house and next to it dug out a rectangular pond and made a rockery.

Soon, Alan had to sit the 11-plus exam. This comprised two examinations to determine whether a pupil went to a grammar or secondary modern school. Alan passed the first part but failed the second. Therefore it was decided that he should attend a secondary modern.

Showtime at Hollyfield Road School, circa 1950

Girls at Hollyfield Road School (Surbiton Central) in about 1950 taking part in a production which involved them wearing Hungarian-style costumes. Among those in the picture are Pearl Vale, who lived in Richmond Grove, Surbiton, and June Shakespeare, whose home was in Hereford Way, Hook.

Hollyfield Road schooldays

HUNDREDS of local children attended Surbiton Central School at Hollyfield Road after the building opened for lessons in 1937.

For the next 29 years, many pupils completed their education at the buildings on the site, just across the road from the Alexandra Recreation Ground.

In 1966, the pupils were transferred to a relocated Hollyfield School at the top of Surbiton Hill Road after a large mansion, White Lodge, was vacated by Surbiton Grammar School in 1965. Now called The Hollyfield School, lessons are still held in the fine old building, erected in 1856 and which still maintains many of its original features.

Alan Davis was 11 years old when he first went to school at Hollyfield Road in September 1948.

The headmaster at that time was Mr F.W.C. Hill, who he recalled was a small, slim, clean-shaven and extremely well-dressed man.

"I believe he was in the army during the war and I think he rose to the rank of Lieutenant Colonel. The way he shouted at us made me think he was still in the services, but for all that, he was a brilliant headmaster and all the kids had a lot of respect for him."

The first class young Alan was put in was Class 1B. The teacher was Mrs Foley, "a lovely, elderly lady who I got on with rather well". Alan was moved up to Class 1A because he often helped the teacher educate less fortunate pupils with reading difficulties. A woodwork teacher Mr "Taffy" Williams was in charge of the form.

"While we all sat on benches listening to him telling us all about mortice and tenon joints, if he noticed us not paying attention, we used to get a rap on our legs with his wooden rule. Most children wore short trousers then until they were about 14 years old, so the ruler hurt. Teachers could hit us then without any qualms.

"At about that time, we had a music teacher called Mr S. Allen. He tried his hardest to introduce us to classical opera with him singing and Mrs Foley playing the piano. As I remember it, the class got out of control as none of us appreciated classical music at that time. I believe he went on to sing opera at Covent Garden."

Alan's December 1949 report shows his class teacher to be

Pat Foster (right) of 83 Middleton Estate prefabs, Hook, Surbiton, with younger brother Roger and their aunt, Hazel Foster, soon after the Second World War. Pat attended Hollyfield Road School during the late 1940s and early 1950s.

Mr Grant, nick-named by the pupils as Goofy Grant. Alan was in Class 2A and was then 12 years old. Although his school reports indicated he was doing well, Alan spent a lot of time off sick with sore throats and it was decided that his tonsils and adenoids had to come out. An operation took place at Epsom and Ewell Cottage Hospital in about 1950.

Hollyfield Road School pupil Pat Foster, left, at the age of 11 in 1946 with a friend, Brenda, who lived in Langley Avenue, Surbiton.

Third form at 'Hollyfield'

Alan Davis' third year at Hollyfield Road School saw him in Mr Peacock's form. "The only thing I can remember about him was that he was a tall, thin man with a bald head and it looked rather like a bird's nest", he recalled while looking back more than half a century at his Surbiton schoolboy days.

"I seemed to be doing rather well at practical subjects and spelling for which I got a mark of 90 per cent. My next report in class A in July 1951 shows a spelling mark of 94 per cent. I think it is still one of the things I am good at."

Mr Hill, the headmaster's remarks at the end of the report states that Alan "has worked well and produced good results. Promising in technical subjects. A keen reliable worker".

Alan's fourth form teacher was Mr Grant, according to his report, which reveals he was not too clever at religious knowledge but above 66 per cent in all other subjects. By July 1952, Alan had achieved a top mark of 97 per cent.

"Among the many teachers I had at Hollyfield Road that stand out in my memory were Messrs Bravery, Davies, Mellon-Grant, Lamb and Mrs Morris, who was the art teacher.

"In July 1952, Mrs Morris submitted one of my paintings to an art exhibition held at Surbiton Library, Ewell Road. It won first prize in my age group. For this I was presented with a book of paintings by famous artists. Many of the paintings were of nude studies. My mother hid my prize from my eyes as she considered the pictures offensive.

"I don't remember when she let me have the book back. I suspect it was when I started to go out to work."

While Alan was at school in November 1949, his grandfather, Grandad Eatwell, died. He had never been a very fit man, having been gassed in the First World War, said Alan.

On 27th January 1951, Alan's mother gave birth to her sixth and last child — a girl called Christine Mary. She was born at 32 Northcote Avenue and provided Alan with his third sister.

"My part in all this was to have to ride the midwife's bicycle back to her home then walk back to my gran's home where I'd been sent once again."

Alan's father, Walter, was working all hours trying to raise the money to feed so many hungry mouths. He toiled away in his garage, repairing chairs for a man called Mr Jelly who delivered the chairs and collected them a week later.

It was at this time that Walter suffered a mental breakdown

Alan Davis, from Northcote Avenue, when he started work after leaving Hollyfield Road School.

and became a "nervous, quivering wreck with no confidence in himself or his ability". Alan believes he never really recovered.

"The doctor sent him to Kingston Hospital where he had electric shock treatment. It partially cured him but I don't think he ever fully recovered." Walter lived for another 30 years, until 1980, despite his condition.

Alan's first job after leaving school was at G.L. Wallis and Son in Pyne Road, Tolworth, just off Red Lion Road.

"I was just the boy employed to make tea and run errands for the men and women," said Alan.

The company made flight recorders for Decca Radar as its main source of business. As a side line, the firm's boss, Mr Wallis, was always experimenting with various ideas.

"I remember one in particular. He devised a roller with lots of dimples along its length and a wheel at each end. This was fitted closely beneath a triangular trough with a handle

attached. When he filled it with grass seeds and wheeled it along, the seeds were evenly distributed along the floor."

It was Alan's job to sweep them all up. Mr Wallis was praised by the staff who wanted to improve their position within the company by associating with him.

"I was only employed there from July 1952 to July 1953. Although it was a very boring introduction to my working life, it taught me that I had to learn to do what I was told by my superiors. I believe he sold the seed applicator idea to Black & Decker. It must have been successful as they are still around today."

On 6th July 1953, Alan started his five-year apprenticeship at the National Physical Laboratories in Teddington, working on machines in its workshops.

"My first foreman was Mr Albert Eaton who whenever he left his office always wore a bowler hat."

Alan cycled to work every day from Tolworth, pedalling through Bushy Park. When he reached 17, he rode a motorbike. It was a 125cc BSA Bantam. His father lent him £75 to purchase it with the promise that he would pay back every penny in time. Its registration number was SPL 653.

At the age of 21, Alan was earning £5 per week.

On 11th October 1958, Alan married Sylvia Nicholls at Worth, near Crawley, and her parents allowed the newly-weds to use their small front bedroom at their home in Crawley.

Alan joined the Royal Electrical and Mechanical Engineers in November 1958 and trained at Blandford Camp in Dorset. Later in his young working life, he moved to Gosport to train to be an armourer. But that is another story.

The Davis siblings: Alan, Jenny, Chris, Sheila and Tony at the funeral of their father, Walter, in 1980.

Headmasters of Southborough School, Hook

School heads John Rook, John Enstone and John Oborn at the reunion in 2003.

THESE four men are known to thousands of schoolboys in the Surbiton, Tolworth and Hook area. They have all held the position as heads of Southborough School, Hook Road.

In the summer of 2003, the school held a reunion party to celebrate its 40th birthday and the incumbent, John Rook, welcomed back former heads John Enstone (1970-1986) and John Oborn (1986-1995).

The school's first head was the stern Mr H.P. Giddy, who retired in about 1970. He had been appointed headmaster of Tolworth Central Boys' School in 1946-7. This school, in Fullers Way, rapidly expanded and an annexe was built next to the the Ace of Spades filling station. This evolved into Southborough in 1963.

Headmaster H.P. Giddy.

Emma and Jabez Summers on their honeymoon in Bangor in 1877. Emma was a postmistress and fell in love with carpenter Jabez, a customer at her village store in Essex. Jabez brought her to Kingston and they had a son, also named Jabez, who was killed, along with his wife, when a bomb dropped at No 6 Ashcombe Avenbue, Surbiton, on 15th November 1944.

Jabez Summers jnr, of 6 Ashcombe Avenue, Surbiton, pictured in the First World War. He and his wife, Mary, were killed when a bomb demolished their home on 15th November 1944. Mr Summers was an ARP warden.

The devastation after the explosion in Ashcombe Avenue. Inset: Mary Summers.

Parents killed as bomb blasts house

Ashcombe Avenue tragedy

AIR Raid Precautions warden Jabez Summers and his wife Mary were the last two people in the borough of Surbiton to lose their lives due to enemy action at home.

A flying bomb — also known as a buzz bomb or doodlebug — hurtled out of the sky on 15th November 1944 and exploded on their home in Ashcombe Avenue. The couple lived at No 6, a house called Overbury, in the road of smart houses between Woodlands Road and Langley Avenue.

Jabez Hugh Hassell Summers, who was 63 years old, and Mary, 65, were both killed as a result of injuries caused by the blast and falling masonry. Mr Summers died at the scene and his wife was confirmed dead later the same day at Surbiton Hospital, Ewell Road.

Mr Summers was the owner of a wholesale builders' merchant's business at 169 London Road, Kingston. The family firm sold fireplaces, drain pipes, sanitary fittings, baths, basins, heating boilers and various water fittings.

Jabez's father, also Jabez, was a partner in a carpentry firm, Golders Merchants, and worked locally in Surbiton and Kingston and the surrounding locality. One day he was sent off to Stansted Mountfitchet in Essex, to help build a quasi-Elizabethan staircase at a house taken over by Spiritualists. This involved staying away from home for a while. Mr Summers snr's wife had died in childbirth while their daughter was being born. This meant their 13-year-old son, Percy, had to go with his father to Essex.

While away from home, Mr Summers snr would send frequent telegrams back home to Kingston. They were despatched from a small post office in the Essex village.

After a while, Emma Hassell, the postmistress — a single woman aged 34 — fell head-over-heels in love with the widower from Surrey. She packed off her widowed mother to a brother in Hackney, gathered her belongings and quickly left for a new life in Kingston upon marrying her new carpenter friend.

The former postmistress persuaded Mr Summer snr that there was little money in being a carpenter. He would be better off starting up his own firm in the building trade. This he did and the business at 169 London Road, Kingston, was founded.

Son Jabez was born in 1881. Jabez jnr later married Mary Oram and eventually took over the family business, which backed on to the railway line at Kingston.

Jabez and Mary had two sons, Martin and Roger. Roger died in South Africa in June 2003, days before his 96th birthday. At the start of the Second World War, Roger was a territorial and was called up. He had trained at the London University as an archaeologist, was unhappy, and in later years went to Rhodesia where there was a promise of a job but ended up as a freelance lecturer. Roger had a daughter, Hilary.

Jabez's other son, Martin, became a bank clerk, serving for a time at Barclays, Ewell Road, Surbiton Hill, opposite Langley Road. He later moved to near Crediton, Devon, to become a dairy farmer with a herd of a dozen Jersey cows and still resided in the town in 2004, living alone, despite being 92 years old.

Both Martin and Roger were away from Surbiton when the bomb fell, killing their parents. Martin, in the Territorials, was an anti-aircraft gunner. He was serving in Palestine when his mother and father were killed. He had left the Territorial Army in 1940 and joined a regiment at Brooklands, Weybridge, before switching to a unit at Farnham. Ten years previously, he had broken an ankle and this prevented him from working as a

An advertisement in 1940 for Jabez Summers' firm.

heavy anti-aircraft gunner. He was subsequently based at Farnham with the 46 Light Anti-Aircraft Regiment, serving in Syria, Egypt and Palestine.

Martin received news of his parents' death in a telegram from his wife, received in Palestine on the morning of their funeral. He could not get home, but brother Roger, also in Palestine, was allowed compassionate leave.

Martin became the father of twins, Jennifer and Malcolm, and a younger son, Nigel. At the age of 28, Nigel was killed in a hit-and-run accident in New Zealand. Malcolm set up home in Banbury and Jennifer married and in the year 2004 was living in Dorchester.

'Mum fainted when hearing Dad had died'
Telegram with bad news

Pat Harman (left) and Maureen Weedon (née Taylor), who lost relatives in the war.

IN the autumn of 2003 a civic ceremony was held at Ewell Road, Surbiton Hill, where a new memorial was dedicated to all the men of the Surbiton borough who lost their lives in the Second World War. Many people had been campaigning for such a memorial for many years including two women who attended the service and who both had a sad story to tell.

Maureen Taylor and her mother, Dorothy, of No 127 Ellerton Road, Tolworth, were staying with Maureen's grandparents at No 55 Fullers Avenue in July 1944 when a telegram boy arrived on a motorbike to say Maureen's father was missing in Italy. Two days later, another telegram announced that Private Harry Taylor, who was serving with the East Surrey Regiment, was dead. Maureen's mother fainted and her eight-year-old daughter returned to Tolworth Infants' School, Douglas Road, next day to be told off initially for missing school.

Pat Harman, of Hunters Road, Hook, was also at the unveiling ceremony. Her brother-in-law, Frankie, a Grenadier Guard, was killed in Salerno, Italy, in 1943. The 21-year-old used to live at No 59 Fullers Avenue. "It broke his parents' heart. They were very poor and they loved their son," said Mrs Harman.

Residents of Beaconsfield Road, Tolworth, staged a street party in 1945 to celebrate the end of the Second World War. Among those in the picture are George, Emily and Gordon Eke, Joyce King, Mrs Kilby, Mrs Baker and Mrs Scott. The three women on the far right are Mrs King, Mrs Willoughby and Mrs Spratling.

Boys regularly caned for misbehaviour

Post-war recollections of Hollyfield

A playground chat at Hollyfield Road School in about 1949-50. From left to right, Lesley Elliott, June Shakespeare, Barbara McRobbie, Pearl Vale, Doreen Wells. At the back is Mary Chitson, who lived in Worthington Road, Tolworth.

VIVID memories of Hollyfield Road School in the period just after the Second World War can be shared thanks to one former pupil — Doreen Wells —who has written down her colourful recollections.

Doreen lived in Douglas Road, Tolworth, and attended the school when she reached the age of 11.

The headmistress, she writes, was Miss F Guyer. Pupils nicknamed her Fanny Guyer. Her subject was domestic science – or cooking to some.

"When in Miss Guyer's domestic science class, we were regularly chastised for using too much water. To wash up a mixing bowl, one was only required to fill it and wash the utensils in it. Never ever run water into the large butler sinks. It was extravagant. Learning to wash clothes and do ironing involved bringing along a small item of clothing to launder. Should one forget, then there would be a shirt of Miss Guyer's nephew to wash and iron. She was strict but fair. Pleasant in a matronly way. After a lesson, sometimes the boys would hang around the school gate to see if scones or rock-hard doughnuts were being carried home by their proud gastronomic creators.

"The headmaster was a Mr Hill, an ex-captain in the army, apparently. His room was situated near the King Charles Road entrance and was elevated from the main building by three stone steps. Here we waited for punishment, should we be seen running along the corridor. The boys were regularly caned for misbehaviour. He was more lenient with the girls.

"A Mrs Morris took art and drama. She was a small, dark-haired attractive woman with interesting spectacles. She was a brisk walker and her dark, curled, shoulder-length hair bobbed as she hurried into school.

"One sports day, she wore the most amazing pair of white cork-soled platform shoes, making her look all of five feet three inches tall. Mrs Morris's drama lessons were held at No 35 Ewell Road, between the fire station and the Methodist Church in a lovely building. Recently it has been used as a drawing office by a local company.

"Miss Byrne taught physical training and netball. She was about five feet five inches tall with grey hair cut short like a man's. Her legs were always well-shaved and stuck out in a bowed manner from beneath immaculate, well-pressed pleated shorts. Above, she always wore a spotless white Aertex short-sleeved shirt, open at the neck. On her feet she had white socks and black, elastic-sided canvas gym shoes. If you could vault the buck and the box, and toss a good netball, you were her favourite. If not, you had to go to the back of the class.

"The school was frequently visited by "Nitty Nora" a nurse from the South Place Clinic in Alpha Road, Surbiton who came to check if we were harbouring any head lice. She was a small and neat person and made us untie our pig-tails and bunches, discouraging long hair. Oh, the shame should one be called back to collect a note from her to take home.

"The music and English master was a Mr Allan. He was a tall, dark, good-looking man with his hair neatly Brylcremed down with a side parting. The boys would rush up to him as he walked down Hollyfield Road daily carrying his music bag. I don't think they were so enthusiastic when it came to sitting in class alongside the girls and having to sing songs such as The Ashgrove, The Mermaid, Tom Bawling and Polly Oliver. All accompanied on the pianoforte by one of our older teachers, Mrs Buree, "a little lady who rode a bike".

"The woodwork teacher was a Mr Turner, appropriately. He was known to the boys as Scummie, possibly because he would use the derogatory term 'scum' when he lost his temper with them. I understand he was prone to throwing things at pupils."

My first boyfriend

Doreen Wells, of Douglas Road, Tolworth, was very sweet on a young boy who had joined Hollyfield Road School in Surbiton, where she was also a pupil.

The lad, who was two years younger than Doreen, was introduced as Victor Ramage and had come to England with a woman known as Mrs Ramage.

Doreen recalled that the boy's real name was Victor Mensel. He used to be a keen cyclist and on occasions pedalled all the way back to stay with an aunt in Germany. His epic journey took him by way of the Hook of Holland. In his panier he would carry coffee, a commodity which was extremely scarce in Germany just after the war.

Friends of Victor understood that his father had been married previously and the boy had a half-brother.

He was born in Flensberg but when the Germans invaded Poland he was sent off to stay with an aunt in Gdansk, Poland.

Victor's family owned a rowing boat and there was great excitement when Doreen, Victor and two friends were allowed to carry the boat a considerable distance from the boy's home to the Thames at Portsmouth Road where they would launch the boat and row to Thames Ditton Island.

The last Doreen and her friends heard of Victor was in the 1950s when he was supposedly living in South Africa and working in the gold industry.

"We had been sweethearts," she said, looking back half a century.

More of Doreen's memories follow on the next few pages.

Doreen Wells, of Douglas Road, and her first boyfriend, a German boy, Victor Ramage, whose real name was Victor Mensel, pictured at Hollyfield Road School.

Hollyfield Road School seen through a fence in the 1940s.

Hollyfield teachers of the post-war period

During the late 1940s, Hollyfield Road School had an exchange teacher from America. Her name was Miss Stephen, Here, former pupil Doreen Wells looks back on Miss Stephen and other post-war members of staff.

"The exchange teacher came from Pittsburgh, Pennsylvania. She had the most amazing clothes. In England at this time, we were still recovering from rationing. Clothes to teenage girls were very exciting and not easily obtained due to finances and a lack of design. So Miss Stephens was a pure delight to behold, in a fine barathea suit with straight skirt and draped jacket in a beautiful soft green or tan – she had two – and always a soft shirt blouse set off with a broach on the lapel. Her hair was light brown and softly curled.

"Our other exchange teacher came from France. His name was something like Monsieur Canvey. He had a look of Freddie Mills, the boxer, about him. Class A1 took advantage of his gentle manner. We had great fun with him.

"Mr Hillman took geography and English. He wore a sports jacket and flannels and was possibly an ex-serviceman. How many others of my age of 14 had a crush on him, I wonder? I sat through geography with a pounding heart.

"One of the older teachers, if not the oldest, was Mr Peacock. He was a portly character in a grey trilby hat and tweed jacket. He strolled around the gardens teaching the boys gardening in a very leisurely fashion. He was a dear man.

"Miss Randall taught needlework and cycled to school. We were all taught to make our own aprons and caps to wear in the cookery lessons. We could keep them at the end if we could afford to purchase them.

"I once made a blouse but Mum could not afford to buy it for me so my cousin, Sheila, who had just started work bought it with part of her salary.

"Mr Grant taught English literature. He was average height, bald, and had a military bearing and a very bouncy gait. He would perch on the edge of his desk when teaching prose. I remember him tapping his ruler to remind us of the rhythm as he recited 'The Athenian came down, Like a wolf on the fold ...' He cycled to school and sometimes took the boys for games in the Alexandra recreation ground. He was a kind and gentle man.

"Miss Hutchings instructed us in maths and science, which

Doreen Wells' own impression of domestic science classes at Hollyfield Road School in the late 1940s and early 1950s. A notice on the wall urges users not to waste hot water.

was the bain of my life. She was a dour Scots matron, with hair pulled straight back into a bun. She was tall and thin. Rarely did I see her smile. She always wore a dark green two-piece suit. She was very strict and a proper 'terror'. To me, she was like a character from a Dennis Potter story.

"There were two temporary classrooms used on the opposite side of Hollyfield Road, sited in the area known as The Fishponds. They stood right opposite the art room and girls' playground. The remainder of that area was out of bounds to the school. Probably the house in the grounds was still in use."

Hollyfield Road School pictured in about 1948.

Ewell Road, near Hollyfield Road, in about 1935.

School snippets, Coopers Garage, Electric Light Works

The main assembly hall at Hollyfield Road School ran between the art room at the north end of the girls' playground and the woodwork room at the south end of the boys' playground. The path which ran between these two locations was out of bounds to all.

Doreen Wells, a pupil at the time, remembers: "My brother and some other boys once called me from the boys' playground, daring me to meet him half way. He had something to show me. So a few boys gathered one side, and a number of girls the other. When I met him in the centre of the path, he handed me a grass snake. I beat a hasty retreat.

"School dinners were served in the Royal British Legion Hall, next to the caretaker's house, *(still standing in 2004)*. The rest of Hollyfield Road had no other houses, as far as I remember. The next building was The Electric Light Works, then, on the corner of Hollyfield Road, where it meets Ewell Road, stood the Cooper Car Garage. I walked past this site four times a day. Sometimes there were mechanics working on racing cars right out on the pavement. Often there lounged a big golden chow dog, with his black tongue hanging out of his mouth. This was an animal to step off the kerb for.

"There were no traffic lights or railings here then. Opposite, at the end of Kingsdowne Road, stood a large old house and a splendid tree surrounded by pavement *(see picture above, right)*. Both these have now gone.

"Between the school playground on King Charles Road and the Hogsmill tributary, stood a little tuck shop at the corner of Beaconsfield Road. It was known to us schoolchildren as Miss Moss's. It was owned by a little plump old lady, Miss Moss, who satisfied all our sweet-toothed needs.

"I remember so many of the old places in Tolworth. There was a brickfield at the end of Red Lion Road and when it was no longer used there was a large pond on the site. We knew it as The Bluey. The Co-op stood in Ellerton Road, opposite Tolworth Park Road and is now divided into three private dwellings.

"At the corner of Bond Road and Tolworth Park Road, Thorogood owned a saw mill used during the war. A small laundry, Longhurst's, stood in Worthington Road before the Second World War. At the end of Ravenscar Road, where it meets Red Lion Road, on the corner was a cycle shop, Hendy's. It was open on Sundays as well as weekdays. At Number 151 Red Lion Road, by Tankerton Road, was a chemist's, Eric Hepworth's, owned by Bidworth Pharmacies.

"At school we would learn country dancing. It was introduced by physical training teacher Miss Byrne. It brought some colour into our school curriculum at last. So out went the instruction: embroidered peasant blouses, if possible with short puff sleeves and low-neck with draw-string. The skirts were ankle-length and gathered at the waist and trimmed with coloured braid. The fabric came from old black-out material.

The long-established firm of H.C. Jones was offering houses in Tolworth for £375 in 1935.

We learned various peasant dances including the mazurka.

Now that we were out of the war years, life was becoming more colourful. Within a couple of years, there was to be The Festival of Britain in London *(1951)* and the coronation of Queen Elizabeth II *(1953)*."

Record producer behind smashes by Elton John, David Bowie, and other major stars

World-famous pop songs crafted by Effingham Road man

THE music industry was in shock in July 2002 when one of the most revered record producers of all time was killed, along with his wife, in a road accident.

Gus Dudgeon lived in the 1970s at No 50 Effingham Road, Long Ditton, a few hundred yards from Surbiton's Victoria Recreation Ground in Balaclava Road.

While in residence in Effingham Road, he was responsible for producing such hits as Goodbye Yellow Brick Road, Candle in the Wind, Rocket Man and Daniel by Elton John. And he was the man responsible for producing 11 of Elton John's albums.

On top of this he produced David Bowie's Space Oddity and scores of other million-seller hit parade tunes known all around the world.

He worked with artists such as Joan Armatrading (who lived near St Mark's Hill, Surbiton, in the 1970s), Lindisfarne, the Bonzo Dog Do Dah Band, Johnnie Bristol, Tom Jones, Ralph McTell, the Strawbs, Ten Years After, Chris Rea, Amen Corner, Gilbert O'Sullivan and XTC. He also engineered John Mayall and Eric Clapton's Blues Breakers album and The Zombies' She's Not There, plus Half Ain't Been Told by Otis Spann featuring Muddy Waters, recorded in 1964.

Gus Dudgeon was the engineer on the 1966 Blues Breakers album by John Mayall featuring Eric Clapton (who was earlier an art student at Surbiton's Hollyfield Road School).

On 21st July 2002, Dudgeon, aged 59, and his wife, Sheila, 63, were killed when his Jaguar car left the M4 in Berkshire in the early hours of the morning and plunged down an embankment. It was not thought that any other vehicle was involved. The pair had been returning home from a party in

Gus Dudgeon and his wife Sheila had a tragic end.

Newbury, Berkshire.

The couple had moved from Effingham Road to Cobham several years previously. Former neighbours at No 48 recalled Dudgeon keeping himself to himself but were aware he was in the music business. Apart from conversations about a boundary fence which needed repairing, there was little dialogue which could have given clues to his fame.

Following the shock news of Dudgeon's death, Sir Elton John led the tributes which poured in from all around the globe.

"I am devastated," he said. "He was an incredibly talented producer and a dear friend for many years. I will miss him terribly."

Rocket Man — one of Gus's hits.

Dudgeon was a colourful character who did not worry about speaking his mind. He wore trademark red shoes and sometimes braces and the frames of his glasses were often brightly coloured.

During his time at Effingham Road his neighbours were stalwart Surbiton Baptist Church members Mrs Nell Passmore and Miss Queenie Laxton, at No 48. Both pensioners were seemingly uninterested in their neighbour's claim to fame.

Another next-door neighbour was Freda White, organist at the same church in Balaclava Road.

Gus was scheduled to receive another industry award two weeks after the tragedy. It was awarded posthumously by the British Academy of Composers and Songwriters.

Elmbridge manual telephone exchange in Ewell Road, Surbiton, in 1965. It became automated in August 1966 and jobs were lost.

Brenda, the little girl killed by a bomb

Nellie Rising and her daughter, Brenda, who was killed by the bomb blast.

JUST three weeks after celebrating her fourth birthday, Brenda Rising was dead. She was fatally injured when a high-explosive bomb ripped apart her home at No 26 Ravenscar Road, Tolworth. Neighbour Mrs Elizabeth Baigent, 41, was also killed. Brenda was the daughter of Arthur and Nellie Rising. She was born on 22nd February 1937. The family's Anderson shelter was flooded at the time of the bomb so Mrs Rising and Brenda were sheltering under the kitchen table. The pair were dug out by ARP warden Albert Creasy of No 16 Hill Crescent, Surbiton. Nellie survived her injuries but spent time in hospital. She was the oldest child of May Midmore, of No 18 Ravenscar Road. Brenda's father was a decorator and was still in England at the time, awaiting a posting abroad. He'd only been away from home a week when the tragedy occurred.

Brenda was buried at Surbiton Cemetery, Lower Marsh Lane. Aunts of Brenda's — Doris Goodchild and Gladys Midmore — also lived in Ravenscar Road.

Brenda's aunt, Gladys Midmore and Ravenscar Road neighbour Beryl Collier in mourning at Surbiton Cemetery.

Surbiton Lagoon

SURBITON LAGOON

The growing popularity of open air bathing in the 1920s led to the opening of Surbiton Lagoon in 1933. It was built on 20 acres acquired by Surbiton Urban District Council in 1930 in Raeburn Avenue near its junction with Alexandra Drive. Here, over the next 40 years, tens of thousands of visitors enjoyed its holiday-like facilities, especially during hot summer weather such as in 1976. In 1934, its first manager, Mr Edward H. Temme (inset) achieved a record Channel swim. He left South Foreland at 6.11am and arrived in Blanc Nez, near Calais, at 10.05pm. The 38-mile swim, on August 19, took 15 hours and 54 minutes. Mr Temme, who was 6ft 2ins tall and weighed 16 stone, was already the holder of the record set in 1927 for being the first man to swim the Channel both ways. The pool closed "for repairs" in 1979 and never re-opened. A housing development was put up on the site.

More Surbiton personalities past and present

Bob Glass pictured in 2004 at Surbiton Station.

BOB Glass was still working as a newsagent in the forecourt of Surbiton Station in 2004 at the age of 85. The town's best-known character began selling newspapers in the town in the 1920s, while helping his father, William Edward Glass. William's link with Surbiton and newspaper vending extended back to 1888 when he was a two-year-old brought along from his south London home to accompany his family selling papers from a barrow in the street.

By the 1930s, the family had their own cabin and in modern times, a shop, which was run by William's grandson, Keith Glass. William once recalled how travellers using horse and carriage to get to Kingston were charged 6d but had to pay 2d more if they wanted to keep their feet dry crossing the stream by Hodgson's brewery. William died aged 57 in 1942. His wife, Edith, and Bob's aunt from Raynes Park helped carry on the business until Bob finished service with the Royal Engineers. William's other son, Bill Glass, became a glazier!

John Green, tea and coffee merchant, moved his business, Traders, to 274 Ewell Road, after 23 years at No 76 Victoria Road, Surbiton. Mr Green is seen here at his former shop shortly before its relocation in July 2004 to the former premises of Yvonne's patisserie.

Mike Batt.

SINGER-SONGWRITER Mike Batt, famed for the Wombles' compositions in the 1970s, plus productions for a whole range of top albums including some by David Essex and 2004 star Katie Melua, lived at 11 Langley Avenue, with his then wife, Wendy, from 1975-1979. He composed Watership Down and co-wrote Phantom of the Opera with Andrew Lloyd Webber.

DAVID ESSEX

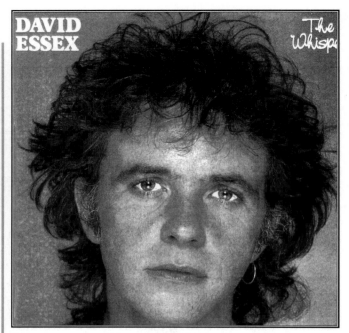

Pop star David Essex

POP sensation David Essex lived for 16 years until 2002 at Glendower, a large late Victorian house at 104 Ditton Road, Surbiton. David Cook was born on July 23 in the hot summer of 1947 at West Ham, east London. He was a descendant of a gypsy family and from a young age took to music, initially playing drums in East End clubs. His crowning glory was his role as Jesus in the rock gospel musical Godspell in the 1970s. During this decade he had seven top 10 hits including two number ones, Gonna Make You A Star (1974) and Hold Me Close (1975).

He was divorced from his first wife, Maureen, with whom he had two children, Verity and Dan, who became his manager.

In 1988, his girlfriend, Carlotta, gave birth in America to twins – Bill and Kit. The boys later moved to Glendower, along with Essex's mother, Dolly, who lived in a flat within the rambling old home after the death of her husband, Albert, in January 1994. The twins are believed to have gone to school in Long Ditton.

In 2004, Glendower was up for sale. The asking price was £1.3m.

Glendower, Ditton Road.

Winthrop House towers above the forecourt of Surbiton Station in this 1960s picture taken in Victoria Road. The offices of the medical drugs company were built in about 1960 on the site of the original Southampton Hotel, constructed when the London and Southampton Railway was opened in 1838. A modern pub was included in the redevelopment. The offices, which were at one time targeted by animal rights activists, were demolished and redeveloped in the mid 1980s after Stirling Winthrop moved to Guildford. In the small parade of shops on the right is the Codeway Driving School. A sign nearby warns the location was an accident blackspot.

Started in 1884

Surbiton High School

SURBITON High School opened in 1884 and was founded by the Church Schools Company, to which it still belonged in the year 2004.

The main school is in The Crescent but in recent years, the school has acquired the Surbiton Assembly Rooms. This has provided the establishment with 10 new classrooms, music practice rooms, assembly and drama areas and a grand dining room in addition to the jewel in the crown – a stage and auditorium with a fine wooden roof.

The boys' prep school occupies a grand old villa at Avenue Elmers, which began life as Arundel House School in the early 1860s.

Part of the main building in Surbiton Crescent was demolished in the summer of 2004 to make way for a modern development of the school. There is also another section of the school further along Surbiton Crescent.

Dr Jennifer Longhurst joined the school in early 2001 from Solihull Sixth Form College, where she was vice-principal. She took over at Surbiton from Miss Perry. A keen linguist, Dr Longhurst could speak fluent French, Spanish and Portuguese. She was also skilled at reading Italian, Catalan and Galician. She had previously taught girls in Sidmouth, Bradford, Leeds Metropolitan University and held a post at Exeter College, managing the academic progress of students.

In her treasured free time, Dr Longhurst said she enjoyed indoor gardening, watching foreign language films and working on her computer.

Some of the girls in 1898.

Dr Jennifer Longhurst, school head.

THE Hollyfield's head in 2004 was Stephen Chamberlain (left). Under his management, he had 1,000 students at the school off Surbiton Hill Road. Part of the site was formerly the grand family home of William Dunnage, built 1856.

Transatlantic Plastics, on the corner of Brighton Road and Victoria Road, pictured in about 1963.

Transatlantic Plastics

TRANSATLANTIC Plastics was a dominant landmark in Surbiton town centre during the 1960s and 1970s. It occupied spacious premises on the corner of Brighton Road and Victoria Road and also another outlet at No 49 Brighton Road.

An extensive range of plastic materials was on sale during its heyday. There was everything from fablon (including woodwork design) to plastic spoons.

The firm's headquarters was not in America or Canada, but in Ryde, Isle of Wight, so perhaps the business should have been called Trans-Solent Plastics!

In the year 2004, the firm was trading from Totton, Southampton, as a medium-sized packaging and polythene supplier and an independent private company.

In the early 1960s, there were a good number of shops in Victoria Road which customers can still remember today.

At No 6 was Puttocks, tobacco and sweets. Freeman Hardy Willis was at No 7. Sam Cook, the fruiterer and greengrocer traded at No 9. In the 1970s, the manager was Maurice Blake who was living near Addlestone in 2003.

Hudson Brothers, grocers, were at No 12 in old-fashioned premises which were retained in later years by Abbey National. MacFisheries were at No 18, at that time occupying a smaller shop with sawdust on the floor and a popular place from which to buy kippers.

J. Rylands, drapers, was on the corner of St Andrew's Road. The premises extended back a long way.

At No 32 was the Kiltie Restaurant, an ideal place to pop in for morning coffee while shopping.

Timothy Whites was a handy place to buy household items such as water bottles and thermos flasks. It traded at No 45. Rogers, the bootmakers at No 68 survived until the 1990s. Obliging staff would offer help if you wanted to buy suitcases or needed shoe repairs.

Did you know?

DURING the heydays of the Swinging Sixties, five local typists came up with a brainwave that would put Surbiton, and indeed the whole country, in the spotlight.

Carol Fry, Joan Southwell, Brenda Mumford, Valerie White and Christine French, who were typists empoyed by Colt Heating and Ventilation Ltd, No 15-19 Langley Road, developed an idea that would lead to them being interviewed by TV reporters all over the world.

By January 1968, Britain was fighting inflation and economic gloom. The five ladies made jaws drop when they suggested that to help the country's plight, the staff work an extra half hour with no pay. The "I'm Backing Britain" campaign was born.

The response was huge. Extra phone lines had to be installed at Colt's by other firms making inquiries. Sackfuls of letters arrived, too.

Prime Minister Harold Wilson was informed of the news and Prince Philip sent a telegram to Colt's congratulating the staff. Across the UK, firms enthusiastically backed the campaign.

An early 1960s' view down Victoria Road, Surbiton. The building on the left, at No 84, is Barclays Bank, which traded for many years next to the station approach. In recent years, the building was turned into The Surbiton Flyer public house. Next to it is the Lankester Engineering Company, at Nos 82 & 83. In the 1930s, it was better known as The Surbiton Motor Works. By 1970 it was called Lankester (Kingston) Ltd. On the far right, Sainsbury's supermarket — later to become Martin's newsagent's — is shaded by a canopy. Also protected from the summer sun is Puttocks, the tobacconist shop, remembered affectionately by many a pipe smoker.

CHRIS Dreja, a key member of the Yardbirds pop group, formed in the early 1960s, attended Hollyfield Road School. One former pupil believes that the band played in the school hall one lunchtime and that Eric Clapton was in the line-up.

TOP boxing coach Fred Barr, well known for his body-building sessions, used to give instruction at Surbiton Lagoon. He lived in Douglas Road. He once represented Northern Ireland in the 1950s and achieved eighth place in a contest, beating Sean Connery.

OTHER memorable characters who attended either boxing, weightlifting and bodybuilding sessions at the Lagoon in the early 1950s included Alan Fung, who later gained the "Mr Hong Kong" title.

And weight-lifter Charles Curzon gained the title Mr Britain in about 1946.

CHARLES Whitnall was a Jack-the-lad character from Lovelace Gardens who as a young man bought up casinos in London and Jersey. He attended the weight-lifting club at Surbiton Lagoon as a young man.

Other books from the same author

Hook Remembered £9.95

Long Ditton Remembered £9.95

Chessington Remembered £9.95

Tolworth Remembered £9.95

Hook Remembered Again £9.95

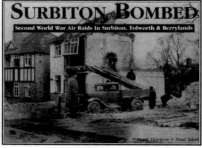

Surbiton Bombed £9.95

Orders

TO order a book by post, please add £1.50 postage and packing for the Remembered Books (above) or £3 p&p for the county books (right). Cheques should be made payable to Mark Davison and sent to North Bank, Smoke Lane, Reigate, Surrey RH2 7HJ.

76

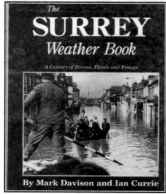

The Surrey Weather Book (£12.95) is packed with dramatic photos and accounts of the county's greatest storms, floods, freezes and hot summers.

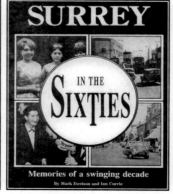

More than 200 photos and stories of the swinging 1960s in Kingston, Tolworth Leatherhead, and other Surrey towns are in Surrey In The Sixties (£12.95).

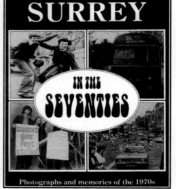

Re-live the days of flares, platform soles, Cortinas and Marinas in Surrey in the Seventies (£12.95). Includes Kingston, Surbiton and Leatherhead.

Mark Davison

MARK DAVISON has written more than 20 books since his first, Surrey in the Hurricane, in 1988 which documented the great storm to devastate the county in October 1987. Mark, who hails from Hook, works as the community editor on the Surrey Mirror in Reigate. His first newspaper position after leaving Rivermead School, Kingston, was on the Kingston Borough News in Surbiton.

Mark says he is greatly encouraged by the tremendous feedback he receives from each new title. His last, Surbiton Bombed, co-written by Paul Adams, provoked a particularly large postbag from which he has been able to secure a number of fascinating tales for this, his latest publication. He says he never ceases to be amazed at the new stories from the past that keep emerging from the Surbiton, Tolworth and Hook areas.

Also available

Kingston Then and Now by Margaret Bellars (1977) £7.95
The Story of Kingston by June Sampson (1972) £7.95
The Story of Esher by Ian D Stevens (2nd edition 1977) £7.95

Please add £1.50 for postage and packing. Further details Tel 01737 221215.